Speaking
for Themselves

Ex-pats have their say

Jan Morgan

CAPE CATLEY LTD

For my family

First published 2008
Cape Catley Ltd
PO Box 32–622
Devonport, Auckland
New Zealand

Email: cape.catley@xtra.co.nz
Website: www.capecatleybooks.co.nz

Typeset in Sabon 10/14.5pt.
Designed and typeset by Kate Greenaway, Matakana
Cover by Trevor Newman, North Shore
Printed by Publishing Press, North Shore
ISBN: 978-1-877340-12-3

CONTENTS

AUTHOR'S NOTE

I MET JOHN CLARKE IN MELBOURNE. TO BE ABLE TO SIP TEA IN ONE OF Melbourne's oldest and most famous hotels and enjoy the pleasure of his company and bask in his wit was indeed a treat.

Spending an afternoon in a Wellington café with Kerry Fox on what was one of the region's most beautiful summer days of all time – well, by my reckoning anyway – was a lot of fun. I felt as if I was meeting up with an old friend.

One of the first interviews I had was with Reg Mombassa, sitting in the attic high up in his large terrace house in inner Sydney with his paintings in piles on the floor or stacked up against the wall. Every now and then he would leap up and rummage through them and bring out a landscape or painting of an Auckland house which especially illustrates his feelings about New Zealand.

I met Teddy Tahu Rhodes one lunch-time in a crowded Sydney restaurant. As I put my recorder on the table between us, the music on the sound system was turned up and other patrons around us immediately raised their voices to be heard. I suggested we go somewhere else, Teddy said no – 'you'll hear my voice clearly enough.' Sure enough, transcribing the tape was no problem: there was Teddy's deep voice booming clearly over the surrounding rabble.

Jon Stevens and I had been trying to get together for a few weeks – he'd been busy touring – when one afternoon out of the blue he phoned me and said he was just around the corner, and to come over. We sat in the park across the road from my house while he told many jokes and we reminisced about Wellington. A charmer, for sure.

Shona Martyn I talked to at the Sydney headquarters of HarperCollins. She has a steady forthright voice broken up with frequent bursts of laughter. I found her charming and friendly – but for a nervous author hoping for a book contract she might be rather daunting. "Exactly!" I can almost hear her say.

This was a very enjoyable book to write. I have met – often by telephone – and talked with a wonderful collection of admirably talented people. I will be forever grateful to everyone who so graciously gave their time to talk on a subject so obviously close to their hearts. New Zealand – their home.

Jan Morgan
Sydney
October 2007

JOHN CLARKE

Even though Fred Dagg's black singlet and gumboots have long since been discarded, John Clarke's wry, dry Kiwi accent is instantly recognisable. His famous alter ego is still so very well remembered. He reflects: "I was looking at some old footage of Fred Dagg the other day, and I'm looking at a man who is younger than my children are now. My children were wandering past and they stood behind me and said, 'You still do that, the way you say that, you still say it the same way.'"

John is an engaging man to spend time with, funny and clever. We met for tea at the Windsor Hotel in Melbourne, a rather grand establishment where his casual open necked shirt and chinos topped by a baseball cap contrasted with the austere surroundings. At a table nearby, a small group of Kiwis kept an eye on us. Once I'd turned off the tape, they came over and introduced themselves. They shook John's hand and one woman thanked him "for all the enjoyment you have provided us over the years". John was clearly chuffed.

John developed the character of Fred Dagg – a reflection on the Kiwi psyche, he explains – after he returned to New Zealand in 1973, following a two-year sojourn in London. Now he is fairly well ensconced in Australia, having moved there permanently in 1977. He places a lot of importance on his environment to make him feel at home. "There are things about where I live, for example, that I can attribute to being brought up in New Zealand. I like living near the sea or a river – I like water, I come from New Zealand."

John Clarke, creator of Fred Dagg, and much more

It was definitely the done thing in the 1970s to leave home and travel to England, to see a bit of the world and to get some work experience. Elsewhere appeared a lot more exciting than staying at home and going stale. And like so many others, John Clarke just wanted to get out, to leave, to go away. "I was bored," he says.

"You weren't 'allowed' on television then. In those days, in the very beginnings of comedy, we had to work in the theatre. There was no possibility of getting into any other medium as they were all controlled by an older generation, and rather boringly so. Nothing interesting happened on any of it, even by accident. But there wasn't much we could do about it. There wasn't a film industry as such, only the stage. So I went to have a look at the rest of the world and I suppose I was waiting, subconsciously, for the wheel to turn a little bit."

While in London he met some "fabulous people and had a wonderful time" but he wasn't interested in living there. "I wanted to work in New Zealand. I didn't want to go away and do it in England, and I certainly didn't think I would stay there. I came from New Zealand and that was the audience I knew, and also I was happier there. On my way back in 1973 I went to Australia for the first time. By the end of that year I was back in New Zealand and Fred Dagg started to happen. By then, too, there was the beginning of a slight liberation about the New Zealand Broadcasting Corporation because there were people of my own generation working on current affairs programmes. If they wanted something funny on the show they knew who to ring. There were several of us and that's how we got going. I stayed there until I came over to Australia in 1977 to live."

Even though John was becoming well known in New Zealand with Fred Dagg, the move to Australia came about partly because of "the way the creative enterprise works in terms of timing – you have an idea and it takes a while to happen and by the time it happens you have another idea and there's a slight disjunction." Doing Fred Dagg was a wonderful experience. "Pretty much unadulterated joy for me, but the NZBC didn't understand how stuff got produced – they thought of themselves as a player of programmes instead of a maker of programmes, and that's no good, that didn't work for me."

So it made sense for him to move to Australia as he wanted to get himself into a position where he didn't have to do the things that didn't interest him. "I needed to find a way to do the things that did, and that would pay enough to live on. So I thought, well, I had to redefine what I did in those ways, which would take a bit of doing as I wanted to write a lot more, We were going to have kids so I wanted to be at home. I didn't want be away a lot."

Family is central to John's life. He married an Australian, Helen, although the idea to move to Australia "was mine, not Helen's. She loved being in New Zealand, but the move was driven by my need to test myself in a bigger place and to make a slight shift in what I did – same tool kit but different job.

"I was very fortunate – I've been lucky so many times in my life. When I was doing Fred Dagg in New Zealand, people offered me work in England, in Australia and, in a couple of cases, America, but I didn't want to do something unless I understood what it was and how I would be able to do it. I didn't want to do it just for the sake of it, or be flattered by the offer. I spend a lot of time with my work one way or another." For John, this meant making sure work wasn't just work, as then it would be hard to be funny at the level he aimed at. "I've done that. You end up doing pretty low-grade stuff because you don't need to do anything better." So the move to Australia was more a question of finding an outlet for his humour to develop.

When he was still in New Zealand he began to contribute to a couple of radio programmes in Australia which had cottoned on to Fred Dagg quite early on – they were playing a lot of Fred Dagg records. "One was the ABC's The Science Show, which is still one of the best radio programmes I have ever heard. When I came here they were my beach-head That's where I landed."

The move worked for him as he found acceptance of his Kiwi style quite quickly. "I think humour is kind of international. When I was a kid growing up I got bits of humour that were French, for example, and I didn't even speak French. I'd see a film in a Palmerston North theatre – you know there were a couple of cinemas that didn't play South Pacific on rotation – and I remember in particular seeing the Marx Brothers movies. I thought – 'Wow, that's not rugby! There's something else in the universe!'

"Of course if you want to be in any creative enterprise, you have to work out what you think, because you've got to work out how your skills work for you. When I was young a lot of the comedians on the radio were doing mother-in-law jokes, which I didn't want to do. If you don't have a philosophy or you're not expressing it, you will certainly be expressing someone else's. I'd got to the age when I went to Australia that I didn't want to do that. Every time you borrow a cliché or nick an idea, you close part of your creative capacity down. You're just storing up other people's material. So I thought I would do better if I took responsibility for what I'm writing and saying, because when I make a mistake, I will learn something."

This philosophy of John's was evident in Fred Dagg. From the beginning he knew his character.

Alter ego Fred Dagg

"He was being amusing and his language was more sophisticated than his ideas. I wanted to concentrate on the structure of the writing. If I'm going to be expressing these opinions as my opinions, then they had better be my opinions and I had better be able to argue them, so I needed to do a bit of thinking."

John looked around his neighbourhood not only for material, but for mannerisms. "I've met lots of people, including members of my own family, who were, say, farmers. They'd be driving by, see someone they knew in the street and they'd stop the car, open the door and get out, leaving the engine running, and go and talk for a year. But there's nothing really to discuss, so they have to find interesting ways to do it. You know, these guys are not isolating radium, they're talking about the weather, so the creativity has to be in the way that it is expressed and that's what has always appealed to me. You need to make part of the observation about the character of the person, and part of it is about the structure of what they're saying."

There were many influences on the creation of Fred Dagg. "Fred Dagg is a kind of collaboration between the audience and me. They're as much in charge of it as I am. I used to listen to the radio. There wasn't TV when I was growing up, so radio was pretty big. But I also knew a lot of funny people at school. I had funny uncles, I liked the funny in things. I was definitely aware when I was at school when adults were talking and one of them was being funny and most of the other adults didn't know it and I'd pick up on it."

11

Did politics influence the direction of his brand of comedy? When he returned from England and found success with Fred Dagg, Robert Muldoon and his National Party were in power. "Muldoon made several attempts at a photo opportunity with Fred Dagg but Fred was always a little busy for that—always a little bit pushed for time when an invitation cropped up. He's not the sort of Kiwi who needed a pat on the back. I didn't particularly like Muldoon, his personality or his policies, or the way that he treated people. I'd never been a member of a political party, so it wasn't particularly a sectarian point, it was just a preference. I grew up watching Keith Holyoake on TV. He spent a lot of time denying he was a pompous clown, which I thought was hilarious."

In spite of the politicians, John values growing up in New Zealand during that time. "It was a wonderful place. I grew up in Palmerston North, and Wellington, and I have a great fondness for those places and the people I went to school with—I knew nothing else. I think New Zealand was pretty happy and it was quite relaxed. The Second World War had finished by the time I was born in 1948 and a lot of people from my parents' generation wanted a peaceful, happy place where nothing much went on."

Like many of his generation, he was taught that New Zealand was God's own country. "It was easy for us to be smug. I'm a beneficiary of the system that flourished in the 1950s and '60s and I'm delighted and proud to be a product of that. I think it is a wonderful place to have come from. When I was a kid I went to the local school just around the corner. Then in Wellington I went to a private school. When I went to university, it cost virtually nothing, and I can't tell you how wonderful it was to go there. These days I would have to do quite a lot better at school than I did then and I'd have to pay quite a lot of money and go into enormous debt. The sort of thing I was doing at university, which is the beginning of what I've done ever since, is not going to look like a very good risk for debt nowadays because how are you going to make enough to pay it back? I was doing every subject that didn't involve numbers, to try to see if any of it interested me, and I'd argue that I was paying for it through my parents paying taxes. That's how the system worked. But these days, apparently, it's clever to put money into an offshore holding trust and have it negatively geared back into your superfund's uncle."

Political encounters overseas were an eye-opener for the 22-year-old student. "The Europeans' knowledge of politics was enormously sophisticated in comparison with mine. We had a country run by a milk monitor and if you got a bad one you were in the shit. A good one and it was bloody marvellous. But there was no other structure. The constitution was written on the back of a packet of Craven A cigarettes with a carpenter's pencil – there's nothing complicated about it. Then a lot of people said, 'Well, we are basically British anyway.' People used to talk about going to England as 'going home'. It was ludicrous."

So – are New Zealanders boring and apathetic, or funny and clever? "Both," John thinks. "I'm all those things. They're not mutually exclusive. I think we are a mix of different things, but when we are most engaged by the human experience, it's not the boring and the dumb part that's being engaged. I think it's possible to appeal to the racist part of the community. People sometimes make statements that are overtly or covertly racist and it's always possible to get some traction when you do that. But there is a kind of balance. The other thing is that not everything about apathy and boredom is bad. I think you can argue there are good things about that as well. You could say they need to be tempered with some things that require a little better of us."

To make a living at his chosen craft, John had to move to Australia. Something that bothers a lot of New Zealanders is that when Kiwis make it big, Australians claim them as their own. This didn't bother John much.

"I think it's quite nice. I hope I'm not so insecure that I think it an insult. With regard to myself and, say, Sam Neill and other people I know and who are contemporaneous with me, we had a great opportunity to access a bigger audience, to move on a bit from being able to do it in your shed, to being able to do it in a Big Top.

"I've always been comforted by the lack of difference in these two countries. I wouldn't want to live in a place that's too different from New Zealand. There are things I enjoy about where I live, for example, that I can attribute to being brought up in New Zealand. A couple of places I love in Victoria, for example, are where it rains quite a lot and they're near the sea." And this reminds him of home.

To move back home would mean having to relinquish work and income. "It would be hard because of my work. If I was suddenly given a lot of money and somebody said 'Here you are, go wherever you like', I think I could quite happily live in New Zealand, but life's not like that. We've got kids and there are a whole lot of considerations. But I could happily live in New Zealand or Australia if I were in a nice place near the coast and had good friends nearby."

He's enjoying the questions he's being asked, John says, but realises he could equally argue the opposite. "Like, for example, it occurs to me that if you go to Australia from New Zealand, as I did, you could regard yourself as being in a type of capsule that gets planted here, but, if you do that, why would you leave? You'd leave if somebody said, 'I'll give you a lot more money to be the bank manager in Wangaratta than you're getting being the bank manager in Hawera', and you'd go, 'Ok, I'll do it.' Well, in that case you're doing it for the money. The reason I came here is not for the money. If I wanted to make money I would never have left New Zealand.

"When I came here I could say 'I'm John Clarke and I was brought up in the Manawatu and Wellington and I'm here to have a bit of a look around – does anyone know any jokes?' You can do that, but you can also come here and say, 'I'm Arnold Smith and I sharpen knives and I used to work in a circus in Canada and my mother was the first woman to win a bronze medal in both the winter and summer Olympics.' You can say anything you like. Nobody cares, because nobody's listening to you. You need to redefine yourself, anyway, as you get older because God forbid you should think the same thing at 60 that you thought at 20.

"So these changes have a metaphorical expression and one of them is place. It can be small or it can be large. The small one for me is remembering the feeling of going from Palmerston North to Wellington, and going 'Oh, this is a bit different – they have trams and the harbour.' It was interesting and different and in no time you are someone else.

"I don't get homesick, not really. I don't think I'm far away. When I was in England, I used to think I was a long way from home, but it didn't stress me much because usually I was drunk when I was homesick. I did

John Clarke looks back on Fred Dagg 1982

Photo: Rennie Ellis Archive

some very stupid things and behaved very badly in all sorts of ways. Everybody does. All I'm saying is we evolve and redefine ourselves by going to a different place. What I do for a living has completely changed me in all sorts of ways but I've still got the same name. I don't want to be the same person I was back then. I hope I've learnt a bit and got wiser. I've been blessed by bumping into some wonderful people in my life and if they haven't had any influence on me, I will be sorely disappointed."

The last time John returned home was 2002. Many of his friends and family come to visit. At first he returned a lot as he was committed to things he had to finish. He goes from project to project. "I'm pleased about a lot of those ones in New Zealand, because I've worked with some terrific people. If I'm happy in myself I see that as success."

One of John's particularly high profile projects these days is the short political satire he delivers each week on the ABC's 7.30 Report, a current affairs show. It's evident in these that Fred Dagg still inhabits him, as if he and Fred Dagg are still in collaboration.

"I see myself doing things that I did as Fred Dagg in 1973 and there is the same stuff in what I do now. I'm not surprised because it's all instinct. Much of what you do is instinct in this business. Fred Dagg and I are part of each other's character. I hear things coming out of my mouth now as if I was Fred Dagg in New Zealand in 1974.

"Yes, I think I am happy. Mind you I'm easily satisfied. Maybe I don't have a very high standard for myself." And he laughs.

Fred Dagg didn't do many jokes. It was more about the timing, delivery and character. John would also add 'language' to that list. "Fred wasn't jocular. I think he had to be un-jocular to have a direct line to his audience. And it's all predicated on your confidence in the audience's capacity to get it.

"I don't think I always did it the right way and some people objected to it, God bless them. There was this uncouth long-haired lout ... I'd like to send a special cheerio to all those people out there who objected.

"The development of my own idea of humour occurred mainly with friends at university. The big influences on people of my generation were the Goons and Peter Cook and Dudley Moore, although there were a great many funny woman who didn't get recognised enough, like Joyce Grenfell, and, particularly, Ruth Draper. Peter Cook – I knew him a bit – would have said, 'You have to speak with your own voice. You won't get anywhere unless you're you.'

"We had so many good influences as New Zealanders. You grow up there and you think – I come from New Zealand. My father was born there, my mother was born there and my grandmother was born there. So why does my foot tap when I listen to Irish music? Why do I like James Joyce so much? There's a reason ..."

John says if it was only money that mattered he could have stayed in New Zealand and worked in advertising. But enlarging on his career was what was on his mind when he left for Australia. "It was very hard to generate a television project in New Zealand at that time, and particularly an imaginative one. I had spoken to a few people who were higher up in television at the time and the advice they gave me was extremely sensible – just not to regard the system I was working in as the only way to do things. It was best to move on while everything was still positive. I don't think I had any notion of what I was going to do in Australia. For the first several months I was just in the audience. I asked myself what was different here. What do I need to learn, and who are these people? It's the traditional migrant experience – you have the opportunity to reinvent yourself. You don't want to be a prisoner of your own success, and you don't want to take it so seriously."

Since arriving in Australia, John has worked on various projects. He has written books, worked in radio, TV and stage, all with great success. The whole gamut. It has been very well thought out. "I have to work in different media because every now and again one of them folds up its tent and moves on. And if they all shut down I'll generate a project where I'll write something such as a family history. I don't need to generate an income in order to be stimulated by writing. A lot of the work I do I do for nothing. No, it's not because I have a lot of money. I'm always working away at something or other, and sometimes it has an income attached to it and sometimes it doesn't, and as long as one of them does it's ok. You see, I do get bored easily. If I was condemned to do one of the things I do, and nothing else, I would enjoy it a lot less.

"I don't think it would matter terribly where I lived. I've always been able to find the plusses in the places I've been in, and the plus with coming to Australia was that nobody knew who I was, and in doing so I've learned different things. I'm using the same instincts and approaches. I've learnt a lot and met some interesting people and had a lot of opportunities here I wouldn't have had in New Zealand."

Most comedians suffer from insecurities. It's hard to see this in John.

RENA 2 OWEN

Rena Owen is a Los Angeles sophisticate. She knows how to do business in Hollywood, and she can hold her own anywhere. Talk to her and it's not long before Rena Owen, "the little Maori girl from the sticks", starts to emerge. She loves to reminisce about her Bay of Islands childhood as one of nine children of a Pakeha mother and Maori father.

While her mother was suffering alienation from her family for marrying someone with brown skin, Rena was already dreaming of travelling the world. Many people don't know that she already had a flourishing career in the theatre as an actor and playwright before she hit the streets of South Auckland as Beth Heke in *Once Were Warriors*. Descended from a Maori chief, Rena is "pretty damn proud" of her heritage.

Rena's Pakeha mother Cynthia was just 17 when she met Kake (Ken). She "scored a summer job in the canteen in the freezing works", where Ken was working. Cynthia's family weren't happy about their involvement. Rena knows the story well. "Everyone was up in arms about it. They didn't like the idea of her seeing a Maori at all, and of course when she got pregnant she was given the ultimatum to adopt this child out and come back to the family or they wouldn't have anything else to do with her." Cynthia dug her heels in, married Ken, and they settled into their own family life.

Rena well remembers Cynthia telling her how, when Ken came to pick her up one time when she was nursing, one of the nurses saying, "Oh, I don't know how you can do it." It was a perfect example of the underlying racism of 1950s' New Zealand. Cynthia said, "The Maori boys in the orthopaedic ward would congregate and have a laugh, and I remember the ward sister would say, 'What could be worse than a lot of silly Maoris.' Even though the government said we had the most wonderful race relations, it wasn't like that." Bringing up nine children without the support of her family was hard, but Ken's family had more or less accepted her, and the children were brought up as Maori under the influence of Rena's formidable Maori grandmother, Nanny Upa. The other great support both Cynthia and Ken received was from the local Catholic Church. They didn't have prejudices. Both were really important in their lives.

Indeed the strong extended Maori family and Catholic upbringing was an advantage for Rena. She says it gave her a very strong sense of whanau and community. "We were very much a traditional family. My mother was a fantastic cook. We had a cooked meal every single night. The closest we got to junk food was fish and chips on a Friday. My mum was a brave woman. I'm quite in awe of her and the life she has had, and, if it ever transpires, I'd like to do something with her life story. I will always regret never having the opportunity of meeting her parents, my Pakeha grandparents.

Rena at primary school, centre of front row

"My father's generation was very affected by 'white was right'. Maori names were changed to Pakeha ones. White was the new way, and in some ways having a Pakeha girlfriend was seen as a status symbol ... well, that's my impression. My mother was a ticket into the new world, and it was probably one of the most defiant things he could have done to my Maori grandmother, getting hitched up with a Pakeha girl.

"Being half-caste we kids were quite a rarity in our town. We had our little primary school reunion a few years ago, and of course a lot of people came home because we had such a tight-knit community. One of the guys made my sister and me laugh. He said, 'Oh, the Owen girls. You were the untouchables!' Certainly there was a lot of animosity towards me because I was neither one nor the other. It was such a dichotomy because when the Springboks came there was a lot of debate at the dinner table. Of course my dad was a big rugby man, and here he is, the brown one, all for the Springboks coming, and here's my mum, the white one, totally against it. I'll never forget her saying to him, 'If it was our kids in South Africa, which side of the street would they walk on? They would have to walk up the middle!'

"My dad was an incredibly charming charismatic character – he was the Maori version of Elvis Presley. I remember at a freezing works social, or maybe a rugby club dance, I just loved watching my parents ballroom dance. They looked fantastic. My mum would be flying around. They were such an attractive couple. My dad was impeccably presented and he prided himself on it, having an hour in the bathroom, while my mum would get ready in five minutes. He was the foreman at the works and a big man in the community. One of my aunties would say that the creases on his trousers would be 'as sharp as a razor'. When he was actually in his coffin, she felt his trousers and said, 'Even in death his creases are as sharp as a razor!'"

Living in Moerewa, Rena went to small schools where everyone knew everyone else. At Bay of Islands College she had an exceptional principal in Frank Leadley, the man she credits for beginning her acting career. "He first put me on stage when I was 15. I was in the Maori culture club and we used to entertain on Waitangi Day or when anyone important came to the school. One year the school was doing *South Pacific* and he said to our English teacher, 'You should audition that Owen girl. She thinks she's a bit of a performer.' Bloody Mary was my first stage role, and the next year I got the lead role in *Calamity Jane* and did a few other community plays."

Even though she felt she had found her niche, acting wasn't encouraged as a career. The choices were limited to teaching or nursing, or for a lot of the girls it was getting married and having babies. "We had no role models as we grew up. Apart from Marama Kingi who read the nightly news, there were no Maori faces on TV. The first to come were in the late 1970s in *Close to Home*. So one of my greatest pleasures was in *Once Were Warriors* because here was a film that tells all Maori kids you can be a writer, actor or filmmaker. We didn't have that. From an early age I always wanted to experience life as much as possible, I remember as a girl lying in the grass while we were milking cows, and looking up at the clouds and dreaming that one day I was going to travel the world. It was just something I was born with. Some people are very content to stay at home and I don't judge them for doing that."

Rena decided on nursing and was one of the last hospital-trained nurses at Auckland Hospital in a class of 66 girls, all Pakeha except for Rena and one other Maori girl. "I went through this enormous culture shock when I started. I'd come from a small town where I knew everyone and where it was predominately Maori, and suddenly I was in the big smoke and I was incredibly homesick. I was a country hick in the city, on the phone every night saying to my mum that I wanted to come home. I wasn't fitting in. I'd been getting top marks so it wasn't a brain thing, but they could see I wasn't too happy. I was taken by the charge sister up to the seventh floor and there was a Maori woman, Sister Solomon, who was the only Maori charge nurse, and she lived up the road from the Nurses' Home. She took me home to have dinner with her two children who were my age. I now had this little Maori family up the road that I could go and visit and have a cup of tea with. Once I qualified as a staff nurse I had really itchy feet. I remember saying to my supervisor I wanted to do my OE, and her advice to me was that if I had the bug I had to do something about it."

Rena left for London in 1982 and stayed for six years. She relished her

Rena living the life in London in the '80s

first taste of what she deemed "freedom" and explored London and travelled around Europe. Exploring drugs came with London's nightlife and her age group. "I was a fool to believe that just because I had School C and UE, and was an SRN, I could play with drugs. Wrong! I played with fire and got burnt!" Rena's year-long drug addiction ended in incarceration and forever changed the course of her life.

She reclaimed the artist within her and wrote her first stage play while sitting in a London prison. "It's really interesting because even though I was in London on the other side of the world I was going through the same kind of spiritual journey that was happening back in New Zealand with Maoridom wanting to reclaim their heritage and celebrate it. It's the very theme of my first play which was later produced and published." Upon her release in 1985 Rena studied at a drama school in London and worked extensively in theatre as an actor and writer.

She returned to New Zealand in 1989 and it wasn't too long before Alan Duff came into her life. "I remember when I read *Once Were Warriors*. I was living in Wellington doing theatre, and when I finished it I thought, 'By God, if that book is ever made into a film, then Beth Heke is a role to die for!' A couple of years later Alan came out with his new book, *One Night Out Stealing*. The publishers were doing a launch and they approached our theatre company to do a reading from the novel. I got this Maori actor lined up and we arranged for him to read a page from the novel, and then on the night of the presentation he got stuck in Auckland. Of course the publishers and promoters were freaking out and I thought, 'Bloody hell, I'll just have to do it myself.' I'll never forget this. Alan had his back to us because he was thinking, 'Oh what a wank. Whoever came up with this?' I started reading and I wasn't that far into it and he turned around and he watched and listened. He came up to me at the end, and said, 'You read that exactly how I wrote it.' He asked, 'Have you read my first book? You'd make a great Beth Heke.' He wrote in a copy of *Once Were Warriors*, 'Maybe my Beth one day. I hope so.'

"A couple of years later I auditioned along with a lot of other actresses, but what I had – and this is the OE for you – I had trained in London, I had years of experience, so Lee Tamahori could see I had the strength, and he could also see I understood the lifestyle. More importantly I had a craft, because it wasn't a role I would wish on just anybody, especially if you didn't know what you were doing. I did *Warriors* in my ninth year as a professional. I'd worked my ass off and I had that hunger to learn   and I've never lost that. You can't just come off the street and do that kind of work. I hadn't lived in South Auckland. No, we were the first family in the north to have a Lockwood home!"

Rena is well aware she could have been a Beth if she had not gone away. It could have happened to her as it happened to so many other Maori, and Pakeha, women. She talks about the years she grew up when Maori were very much second-class citizens. "Even we Owen kids, we were half-caste and we grew up with an inherent inferiority complex. I remember taking Maori as a subject in high school and being taught by a Pakeha and in my young mind it didn't make sense because for my dad it was his native tongue, but the only time we ever heard him speak it was with our nanny or on the marae. I remember going home from school, saying, 'Dad, why aren't you teaching me?' He said, 'Never mind. Just get your School C, and your UE.' They did what was right for us, because back then learning the language wasn't going to get you a job. Of course his generation and his mother's generation had the language whipped out of them in schools, and they were forced to learn English, so it was pretty much a dying language." She explains how her generation missed out. Even though they were regularly on the marae they were never encouraged to speak the language.

Warriors premiered in Cannes in May 1994, and didn't get to Sundance until 1995. Along with the impact it had on the New Zealand cinema, Rena found herself caught up in "an enormous whirlwind". It took her a while to comprehend that her life was never going to be the same. "You go on this frantic trip around the world to all these festivals and interviews. I got to understand how the international market works. I was able to forge good relationships with investors, distributors and film festival directors. Towards the end of it I felt I needed to be grounded and go back home, back to where I began which was the theatre. It was intoxicating and I could see how a lot of people get caught in the cycle. Thank God there was that more sensible Kiwi side of me to bring me back to the nuts and bolts that got me there and think about the craft of acting.

"One of the first project offers I got after *Warriors* was a Cindy Crawford film. I can't remember what it was called and it bombed, just like I knew it would. Why should I act in them just because it was Hollywood? I just kinda knew that my second film would be more important in some ways than the first one. I wanted to hang on to my artistic integrity. I eventually chose *Dance Me To A Song*. I knew I had made the right choice because the buzz was once again that I'd had done something good. I didn't want it to be a movie that had died in the box office, or one that went straight to video. Although I'll be brutally honest and say that, now I'm older and I'm more secure in myself, and my integrity has been secured internationally, I'd take the big pay cheque. In your 20s you can do the poor artist thing, but I'm now in my 40s and it's different. Not that I'd do a really bad film, but I think when you get older, like it or not, money does become a consideration."

Rena received no fall-out from *Once Were Warriors*, apart from one Maori who, while a bit under the weather, approached her in a restaurant. He was angry she had made his wife cry. But the reactions from women who have been in Beth Heke's position and have approached Rena have been too many to count. "It's shocking. What did surprise me was the Pakeha women who told me they have lived that life – and these women weren't necessarily working class!"

Living in Los Angeles has its advantages and disadvantages. "I'm here on a mission, so to speak, and my plate is full in terms of work. I don't have time to indulge in missing home and I never feel disconnected. My

Rona in Santa Monica

home is in New Zealand and I go to school in Los Angeles and that's how I see it. America will never be my home. Even if I pretend it is, it won't be. It's an incredibly different culture. Being here is an occupational hazard. If you are serious about making films in whatever capacity, this is the capital of the film-making world. I can never have the same learning opportunities in New Zealand. When I was offered another film here I was really torn about making the move because I had a great life back home living on my nanny's farm. I said to Mum, 'I've got everything I need. I've got a great family and friends.' She said, 'Listen, girl, there are thousands of little Maori girls out there who would love to be in your position. We will always be here, but you will not always be able get on a plane to live and work in LA.' She was right. You've got to take these opportunities. I'm glad my mum gave me the nudge.

"As an actor you're hot for only so long, and at the time you think it's always going to be that way. I often get juicy roles come my way, and I still feel there are a couple of great roles for me out there." Rena was already in her early 30s when she made *Warriors*. Another consideration too was that she was launched in an ethnic role, which confused some in Hollywood. "I would go in and do my auditions and they would say, 'Well, she was great but what is she?' I remember the New York review in 1998 of the New Zealand film I did, *When Love Comes*. The first line said, 'If Rena Owen was as white as Cate Blanchett or Gwyneth Paltrow, she would have done a lot more by now.' It's a fact. I know I'm a good actor and give me good material I'll know what I'm doing. But it's about a look, and it's, well, I look the way I look.

"My mum has said to me, 'Just remember that Judi Dench didn't get her break until she was in her 50s.' I think what I've learnt from being here is to be secure in who I am. The first year I was here I'd go into auditions with all these gorgeous creatures, and granted a lot of them have had a lot of work done on themselves, but I'd feel very intimidated and think, 'Oh my God, is that what I have to do to work in this town?' You've got two choices – you can buy into it or ignore it. I had enough money to set myself up, but not enough for surgery! The thing that kept me going was I could never go back to New Zealand looking like Joan Rivers," and she laughs.

By the end of her first year in Los Angeles, Rena admits she hated it. There was the ever- present pollution and the constant chore of trying to get the Americans to understand her Kiwi accent. But she quickly came to the conclusion that LA was not going to change just because she had moved there. She began to focus on her work and made the most of it. "Maybe it's me and my rural background, but I've never lost my sense of being down to earth. Sam Neill said it well – that we are the country that invented the word modesty, which in LA doesn't serve me well because this is a town that blows its own trumpet, and I'm just not comfortable with that. I think we are more a country that lets our deeds speak for themselves. It's a big part of us. New Zealanders have wonderful work ethics. In London Kiwis do the menial jobs the British wouldn't do. I remember scrubbing toilets to pay my way through drama school. I didn't care. It was just a means to an end. We're not snobby in that way. We'll get our hands dirty. I still think that is part of our pioneering spirit. The Americans love to employ New Zealanders. We do what needs to be done, and I love that.

"We're resourceful and we use our ingenuity. The Americans buy everything, but we don't waste, we conserve. It's quite heartbreaking here – this is the land of extreme waste. Even these chi-chi functions I go to, with all the thousands of dollars spent on one premiere, and at the end of the night a lot of that food is thrown away – it's the land of waste. The things they celebrate – it's extreme, it's ostentatious, and what it has done to Americans isn't right. They live with a debt mentality. It's the only country where you have to be in debt to have good credit. I'd always been a cash-only girl, but here you have to have hire purchases and credit cards. The mana is money. I've see people who will not drive their car on to the lot because it's a couple of years old. We don't define ourselves by that. My whole life is not based on where I live, and what kind of car I drive.

Rena with Temuera Morrison

"Of course this modesty is a double-edged sword because on the other side of it we have the tall poppy syndrome. If somebody does really well, we want to cut them down and put them back in their place. I think both Australia and New Zealand still suffer from the colonial chip on the shoulder. We don't celebrate our successes enough. When I did *Warriors* I was at the top of my game, and some people at home wanted me to do another film, but the financiers said, 'You can't use Rena Owen, she's Beth Heke.' Any actor will tell you that if they've had a hit, they will always be defined by that role. You know what – I was just an actor. I wasn't a victim of domestic violence. I didn't even have children. I was playing a role."

Rena talks about the resurgence of the Maori language and culture, something she says she's very proud of. "It's really awesome now to hear it being spoken everywhere. Its great knowing that kids today don't have to grow up with that inferiority. They're now feeling proud of who they are and what their heritage is. When I was nursing in Auckland I had to do three months on a geriatric ward, I had an old Maori man on my ward, and of course I went up and said, 'Kia ora,' and he looked at me and said, 'Don't you dare say that to me!' It was something that people were made to feel ashamed of."

She doesn't see herself as a radical, more a moderate person, though she feels radical revolutionaries need to be out there to spearhead change. "I'm pretty damn proud of Chief Kawiti of whom I'm a direct descendant. One of the first to sign the Treaty, he got a lot of flak and was accused of selling out to the British. In his speech he made at the time of the signing he said, 'The day will come when you will become labourers under your Pakeha friends. Await, therefore, until the sand-fly nips the pages of the Book.' (i.e. The Treaty). 'Then, and only then, shall you arise and oppose.' Which is so visionary. Well over a hundred years later the Treaty was finally recognised as a legally binding document.

"I've never forgotten Dame Whina Cooper in the 1970s when she did the land march to reinstate the language. What is the culture without its language? We've come a long way and we've still got a long way to go. Why didn't they allow the Maori flag to be flown from the Auckland harbour bridge on Waitangi Day? I'm really surprised that a piece of material could be that threatening, but as a nation why can't we celebrate it? Like it or not, the history of Maoridom is part of that land. What makes us distinctive is our cultural heritage. The sooner we grow up and say this is who we are, the better, and until that day comes we will always suffer with the tall poppy syndrome, or the 'colony chip'. I consider myself very lucky to grow up with my Maori culture."

Rena has a personal celebration every time she returns home, indulging in the luxury of clean air and good seafood. There are some other changes she notices as well. "I don't say this in a negative way, but the past few times I've felt a bit perturbed after being in Auckland. It's felt as if I was in Hong Kong. I did a film in Queenstown a while ago and there were no New Zealanders running shops – they were all Asian or English, and I wondered where the Kiwi kid was going to earn his pocket money. But you can't stop it. They're a cog in the evolution of our country and I do love it that Auckland is full of so many diverse cultures. I really can't wait until I can live down there full time."

Talking about what is unique to New Zealanders, Rena has no hesitation in describing how good it is to meet another Kiwi on her travels. "No matter where you meet each other in the world, there is an affinity we have with the land itself. We all have this very strong pull back to those two small islands. I grew up knowing the story that when God made the world he made New Zealand for himself. I think we are a special bunch of people and we need to find our self-esteem, our worth, and be proud of it. There may be a lot about American culture I dislike, but there is one thing I think about this country that is true, and that is that it doesn't matter who you are and what you are if you are willing to come here and work hard and make a lot of money. They celebrate success, they are not intimidated by it, they aren't embarrassed or shy of it. They celebrate it. One day that is something we'll be able to do."

In 2003 Nicola Scott, daughter of Christine Cole Catley, introduced Rena to the novel *Behind The Tattooed Face* by Heretaunga Pat Baker, published by Cape Catley in 1975. Most impressed, and with the permission of the author's estate and the publisher, she optioned the novel. For the last five years, with the assistance of the NZ Film Commission, Rena has been working on the project and "It's developing into the epic screenplay. It's a pre-colonial tale of power, love, and war. It's a national taonga, treasure, and I feel honoured to have been entrusted with it …

"I think Maori have a quality that can often turn destructive, as in Jake the Muss. We may not have survived without it. It's well documented that the British had never come across natives like us. Everywhere they went they either wiped out an indigenous population or at least subdued them, and then they met the Maori and they got 30 years of the Land Wars. So ultimately it was, 'If these buggers aren't going to back off, let's all sign a treaty.' I've often talked to my Maori colleagues about why we are so aggressive, but consider the weather. They had come from hot climates and then they were in New Zealand up against freezing rain and wind and incredibly rugged terrain that they had to conquer. They weren't having the easy life. I think there was that survival spirit that was born while they had to conquer the vast Pacific Ocean and adapt to this new land."

The most formative time in her life was her rural childhood, which made her the kind of woman she is now. When she was back in New Zealand in 2000 doing a theatre piece playing a Maori woman for the International Arts Festival, she did an interview for one of the papers. "It made me cringe a bit," she says now. "I felt like ringing up the journalist after the article came out, but I thought, 'Oh well, it's just naiveté on her part.' She had written something like –'Here's Rena Owen who lives in Los Angeles. We will now have the opportunity to see if she has held on to her Maoriness.'

"You know, being a Maori is not something you take off and put back on. It's part of who I am. I don't put it in the wardrobe and forget about it. It's the essence of how I grew up, and who I will always be. My background enabled me to go around the world because I am very clear about who I am and where I come from."

REG MOMBASSA

REG MOMBASSA'S AUCKLAND CHILDHOOD HAS REMAINED CLOSE TO HIS HEART throughout his life. Photos show a happy, carefree little boy blinking innocently into the Papakura sunshine. "For us boys the ultimate weapon of choice was a slug gun. I badly wanted one but my parents realised that I was an idiot and refused my request. My friend Warwick had one, though, and we managed to do many foolish things with his gun.

"One of our games consisted of riding your bicycle swiftly past the designated firing range between the house and garage, while one of the boys fired at you with the gun. It was great fun while it lasted. Although we managed to avoid any serious injuries, one of the boys from a neighbouring primary school was blinded in one eye by a slug gun, so the local headmasters ganged up on us and severely discouraged their use." Perhaps not quite so innocent.

New Zealand in the 1950s was a time when Reg, his brother Peter and the neighbourhood kids roamed newly developed semi-suburban Papakura with nothing to fear – except for themselves. "I think the risks we took then were fairly normal for that environment. I'm sure my children have risked their lives in many different ways that we haven't noticed or been informed of," he says now.

Reg's mother Trudy immigrated to New Zealand from Manchester, England, by herself, after having being let down at the last minute by a friend who was going to accompany her. Facing the daunting task of arriving in a strange country on her own wasn't going to put her off. It wasn't too long before she met Reg's father, Jim O'Doherty, from Offaly in Ireland, when they were both working in a psychiatric hospital in Auckland.

"Mum always said she was glad she left England because we wouldn't have had much of a chance as working-class boys in the English class system if we had been born over there," Reg says. "Mum just loved New Zealand. She thought New Zealanders were fantastic. They had a good education system and weren't subject to a rigid class system.

"My father was a lapsed Catholic – he hated that strict Catholicism he was brought up with. I guess because of that I have a slight distrust of the upper-middle-class and it has had an effect on my personality and my work – I like to reflect that disrespect for authority and for big institutions like the church. I am a nominal Christian. I don't go to church, but I was brought up as Church of England, so that Christian culture is part of my outlook as well. A lot of my art is about that. I believe Jesus existed but I don't believe in all the dogma that the churches have made up to make their new religion more impressive and entertaining. I can deal with all of that through my art, in a humorous way, of course.

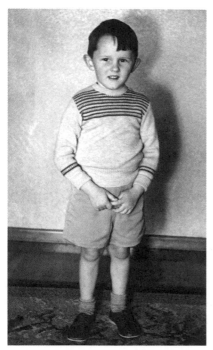

"Dad did a carpentry course when he arrived and started working as a carpenter, building houses around the Papakura-Takanini area. When I was 11 we moved up to Whangaparoa where for about three years Mum and Dad ran a motel, which Dad built. I think they just wanted a break from the building. It was on 10 acres of scrub and bush with a bit of an orchard. We would sell the fruit every year and I'd sit out on the road with a box of peaches. We loved it – it was a pleasant rural existence with nice

Reg at four years old

weather and nearby beaches."

It was while he attended Auckland's Westlake Boys' High School that he thought about painting for a living. "I was pretty useless at anything else. I wasn't good at sport and I wasn't particularly academic, so art was what I really wanted to do. But I also got into playing the guitar when I was about 15. The rugby boys would tend to pick on the kids who hung around the art room, but our teacher was aware of that and tended to stick up for us. The physical education and technical teachers would pick on the art teacher because they didn't like him or his slightly sissy students."

In 1968 when Reg was 17 the family moved to Australia, leaving a recession behind. "Mum and Dad had built a spec house and it took months and months to sell so they thought they would try their luck in Australia, which was booming at the time. They hadn't been to Australia before so they just took a punt on it, really." Reg can't recall any family discussions about the move. "That was what they decided so that was what we were going to do."

Reg says he wasn't very pleased about the move. He was sad to leave his friends behind, and found it strange getting used to Australia. "It seemed like America – everyone had a different accent and the cars were bigger and they drove faster and it was really hot. But I got used to it. Working on a building site I was teased about my accent but it was pretty good-natured. It wasn't spiteful. I mean, lets face it, Australia and New Zealand are pretty similar culturally, and have a similar sort of racial mix. I had a pretty broad accent that I couldn't hide – in fact I still haven't got rid of it, which is surprising. Apparently when I first went to school as a young child I had a broad Manchester accent. We had my Mum's sister and her husband and children living with us for a year or so when they had came out from England, so I had been brought up with all their accents. Mum said my accent was very broad northern England, but after about three months of school I had developed a pretty broad New Zealand accent," he explains with some satisfaction.

On the other hand, he wasn't altogether unhappy about leaving New Zealand. The social life in Auckland for young people was quite violent, or at least it seemed that way to him. He was beaten up a couple of times.

"Maybe it was my fault. I might have been a cheeky dickhead, but I did cop a few hidings and it did worry my mother. I'm scared of violence so I was glad to leave all that behind, but then again I got beaten up over here, too – I must have one of those irritating faces!

"I think being here probably did make a difference to my art. New Zealand has good art schools like Ilam in Auckland. I was thinking before I left that I'd go there, but New Zealand is a small place and the opportunities here in Australia are better. If you are a musician or an artist you have got to come here, or go to America or England. Because New Zealand is such a small country, you can exhaust the audience pretty quickly."

When he first arrived in Sydney, Reg's mother sent him into town to get a job as a commercial artist. After viewing his work they advised him to enrol in art school, which he did, but after a couple of years he left and got a job labouring. "Then the Whitlam government got in and they set up a student allowance, so I thought I might as well go back to art school and get $43 a week from the government for drawing some pictures. That's also when the Mentals – Mental As Anything – got together. It was in 1975, and I had my first exhibition that year as well.

"Yeah, it was a big year. I also met my future wife that year."

After Dare Jennings, the creator of Mambo clothing, saw a record cover Reg had done for the Mentals – it had a couple of chooks running along, vomiting blood – Jennings asked if Reg could design something similar to go on board shorts. After the first design success he was asked for more, and ended up in the enviable position of designing whatever he liked, with Mambo taking their pick. "I did some stuff connected to surfing and from then on I kind of referred to it now and again. In some ways Jennings was a bit of a patron of the arts, and not only to me. He gave a leg up for other artists as well. It's a wider exposure than an artist would get from, say, just showing in a gallery. I've always worked as a freelance artist for Mambo. A lot of people think I own the company and they send me letters asking for jobs and huge donations for various charities and political things. It's just the public's misconception about it all – no, I'm just one of about 10 or 12 artists who have regularly contributed."

Reg (left) with Mental as Anything

The Mambo shop in Sydney's Paddington opened in 1995, featuring one of Reg's designs on a long narrow banner out the front of the shop. This caused a minor stir. "It was an Australian Jesus, naked, but he had a robe wrapped around him. He was slightly overweight and he looked a bit gay, so I guess that would have offended some people. Anyway these guys walked in and hassled the shop manager and I felt a bit guilty about it because she had to put up with the hostility. Anyway they never showed up again. I think they'd come from a local football match."

When Mental As Anything became more popular, they started writing their own songs and signed with a record label. They began touring around Australia and Reg found he was juggling his art with his music. "We just thought we were going to be a fun art school band that played our favourite blues and Rolling Stones songs, but it developed a life of its own."

After years of touring, Reg left finally about six years ago along with his brother Peter who had also been in the band from the beginning. "In the last 10 years it hadn't been full time, but we were constantly going away. I did a lot of the Mambo work as we toured. I painted in motel rooms. Peter did too. He's an artist in his own right as well, and we took our stuff with us everywhere. Sometimes I'd paint in oils, which can be pretty bad when you're trying to clean up in motel bathrooms! I always took photographs as we travelled and I would often draw in the car – if I wasn't driving, I was drawing. In a way it was good because you could be a part-time artist as you were touring in a rock band."

Reg goes on to discuss his odd name. It is an alias which, when invented, quickly took on a life of its own. "It was just a game that the band members had. We would think up stupid names for each other, then after a few weeks think of something else. The idea for Reg Mombassa came to me when I thought I would have a really plain truck driver's name for a first name and then an exotic foreign one for a last name. I thought it was funny, having a mismatched name. Once my father did say to me he was a bit disappointed that I had got well-known with a fake name instead of the family's. But then again my brother, in the band as well, used his real name. Anyway I never made it a secret that my real name is Chris O'Doherty. I started using the Reg name around 1977. I gave it to a journalist or record company and I kind of got stuck with it. I use the other name sometimes but you just confuse the public so I just stick with Reg."

He says he's not sure whether his humour is from any particular way of thinking; it's more a combination of ancestral heritage. "It's the Irish humour from my Dad's side, if anything. If you ask who else I have been influenced by I'd say by Flann O'Brien, the humorous Irish writer – very funny sort of surreal kind of spiritual absurdity. I find that very inspiring."

Reg thinks the New Zealand and Australia senses of humour are quite similar. "Australia has a self-deprecating thing, and also a tradition of mocking authority and pompous people, and that's kind of important to me in my work. New Zealand has that, too, but I think Australians are probably a bit more cynical with it. I remember once when we played at a concert about 14-15 years ago in Auckland, and Stevie Ray Vaughan and a few other American artists were playing as well. Backstage there were the New Zealand roadies and crew, and a couple of old New Zealand friends had come along. It struck me then that I could see that difference between the two countries. It's an almost naive enthusiasm of New Zealanders, it was there backstage – a sort of energetic almost belligerent innocence. I can remember festivals we did in New Zealand and the Australians in our band being quite fascinated by the bikie gangs, lots of scary-looking Maoris lolling around in the sun. It was pretty funny but also slightly scary."

Reg with one of his Mambo paintings

Reg keeps abreast of the political situation in New Zealand and says he's proud of the way New Zealand has behaved politically in the world lately. He talks of the political difference between the two countries. "New Zealand has been quite independent-minded with its own foreign policy, whereas Australia hasn't. There is a big difference in the two governments. If that changes and it gets too unpleasant here, I can always go back to New Zealand. Although that'll probably happen and they'll get a conservative government in, so you can't win really!

"New Zealand's government appears to take a more generous attitude to asylum seekers, but, having said that, I think it seems more left-wing, and I hope that keeps going. I've noticed the reaction to the Waitangi Treaty pay-outs – they needn't chuck out the baby with the bath water, and they need to be careful they don't vote against it all. It was different when I was younger. Now Maori seem to have some respect and more political voice. When I was a kid they were just the indigenous people. They got the crap jobs."

Reg enjoys talking about painting. For a while he was finding it hard to find something to paint. "I had already been here a few years, I was 23 by then, and I was sort of trying out different things and I thought I'd try something more personal. I was thinking about being a kid and how the world seemed simpler then. Everything is remembered as a sort of psychedelic fairy tale with some sort of romantic spiritual aspect, particularly in dreams. I was looking at these black and white photos of the first houses we lived in in Papakura." Inspired by this, he began to produce the paintings that became part of his first exhibition. "I was making up the colours. I couldn't afford to go back to New Zealand at the time, so I couldn't see the actual colours. It ended up that I was painting them from memory, making up the colours and painting the beautiful shining white of the sun on the weather boards and fibrolite against the rich New Zealand landscape."

These paintings didn't come about from homesickness; they were simply fond childhood memories. "It was also an aesthetic thing as well. Now when I think about it, it must have been great for my mother, living in one of those Papakura houses, as she grew up in a working-class suburb in gloomy Manchester and ended up in New Zealand living in a sparkling white house. So that memory of New Zealand is very important. It's funny, because sometimes when I do Australian landscapes I colour them in with New Zealand colours. It's very important where you grow up. Your local landscape is integral to your early memories, and much as you might change and go to other places, it stays with you. Well, it has with me."

Although Reg has an Australian passport he still considers himself a Kiwi. "In an official way I'm an Australian, but I still consider myself a New Zealander from having being born there and spent my childhood there. But I've been in Australia for around 30 years and I have an Australian family, so I probably would have difficulty making a living in New Zealand. I guess you could say I'm an Australian who is a New Zealander! I'm not particularly nationalistic. If I hear a New Zealand

Reg and his cat, Puss, 2006

accent I'm vaguely interested, but it doesn't mean I'll speak to them – but it's like you are always aware of it. I think it's partly that you come from this tiny country at the bottom of the world, which is a long way from anywhere, and in terms of cultural influence on the world, it has nothing. Maybe that's changing now and people are noticing New Zealand for various reasons.

"I think that if you are at the end of nowhere it inspires you to try harder and do something, but it can give you a chip on your shoulder which can also be very interesting. Of course there is the healthy outdoors lifestyle, not that I particularly related to that as I was usually in my room listening to records and reading books like a nerdy sissy. It seems to me that both Australia and New Zealand have a peculiar youthful energy, if that is the right way of putting it. Australia and New Zealand now look attractive because they both have small populations. They are politically stable and there's the beautiful weather – it must seem like paradise to a lot of people around the world. I hope they don't all come and take it from us. America might one day say, 'All of you out. All our old people are coming to live here, and every one of you can go back to Europe or wherever else you came from!'

Over the years Reg has been back to New Zealand, touring with Mental As Anything, seeing family, or visiting the Auckland Mambo shop for promotional work. He enjoys being back among the memories. "I feel quite nostalgic – the accent, the rain. Sometimes I wonder about living there again, but it would be a hard thing to do because – there's no history there for my family. It's all my history – but I admit I have tossed it up in my mind."

He says it's different from how it was when he was a kid, but it's still the same landscape, "and that's kind of comforting in a way. I think there're still some very conservative pockets in New Zealand – maybe it's that English conservatism that is still there. After all these years I always barrack for the All Blacks. I tend to support the underdogs. It's exciting when they perform the haka but I don't think I ever did one when I was a kid. I've always found Maori humour and enthusiasm really inspiring. I wouldn't consider myself politically correct. I can make some really coarse and oafish jokes, but it's something I do support. But you've got to remember the basis of political correctness is treating people with respect, and particularly people who have been treated badly in the past, like Maori and the Aborigines.

"New Zealand used to be a slightly racist country, but that seems to have broken down now. Maori needed to be compensated and be treated better, but you've got to be careful not to go too far either way. The more aggressive and radical Maori element that says they want all whites out of the country – but that's not very realistic. Hopefully the influence of the kids who have grown up in this new era will dominate. A couple of people over here have said to me recently that I had a New Zealand personality, but I'm not too sure what that means. It's a good way of teasing people, though, but I can give it back. I've got fairly good eyesight but I need glasses for seeing in the distance and I rarely put them on in

Australia. When I would go touring with the band to New Zealand I'd put them on and I told the guys it was because the country is so beautiful. I said I didn't need them in Australia because the country is so ugly. I was constantly teasing the Australian guys in the band about how great New Zealand is."

Reg has never considered an alternative design for the New Zealand flag. "But I've thought about the Australian flag a lot. My plans for that would be a blowfly or a really bad pencil drawing on a white flag – if anything maybe a bit of grass, or something. There is a painting I've done with a Kiwi and a kangaroo connected by a chain. It's called 'Metaphorical Proximity'.

"In 2005 I was asked to open the Colin McCahon show at the NSW gallery. Sometimes when they ask me to do these things I try to get out of them, but because I was interested in McCahon's work I did it. I think he was a great artist and his paintings triggered a lot of feeling about New Zealand and its landscape. I'd say he's had a direct influence on my work. I do admire him. New Zealand does breed some interesting people. It's produced some fantastic rock bands, maybe because there is nothing else to do – play guitar while it's raining outside. There is a definite style and that is probably influenced by the Maori and Pacific Islanders' approach. You know the beat they used to call the Maori strum – I use it all the time.

"I'm always saying to my kids, 'You're actually New Zealanders, I'm going to take you to live in New Zealand.' Once one of my daughters said, 'Oh, New Zealand is the land of nerds!' You can see why an Australian would say that. I think she was referring to the broad accent!"

ALANNAH CURRIE

ENVIRONMENTAL ACTIVIST, SINGER AND ARTIST ALANNAH CURRIE SAYS SHE GREW up "never having a sense of myself as a New Zealander". Leaving New Zealand in the late 1970s for London, she climbed to icon status with the band Thompson Twins. It was only when she returned to live in Auckland with her family in 1993 and lived there for 10 years that she discovered her roots, and made peace with her Kiwi identity.

"There was an excitement in the arts and people were looking at themselves and talking about where the nation was going. I was curious, and wanted to be part of that." Now living back in London she finds it hard to let go.

Alannah Currie was raised in a fibro state house in Auckland's Mt Roskill, the youngest of five children. Her father took off when she was just five and her mother was left to raise the Currie children on her own. "My father was actually a gambler and an illegal bookie. That's what he did when he wasn't working at the freezing works. He rarely gave my mother any money so we got by on what little she could earn as an office worker, and whatever we could grow in the garden." In spite of having no money, Alannah says she had a really happy childhood. "There were lots of fields round Mt Roskill in those days and I remember gorgeous summer days exploring creeks and playing in trees, building huts and roaming the neighbourhood with gangs of barefoot kids, and only coming home when it was tea time. We seemed to be forever making something – cakes for letterbox stalls, party dresses and hats, or trolleys out of broken pushchairs.

"I was very lucky to have a Maori family who lived next door whose father I semi-adopted as my own. I was fortunate to get a great bi-cultural upbringing at a time when New Zealand was still a very racist society. On the weekends I would pile into the back of their old red truck with all the other kids and the aunties and we'd roar up to Ninety Mile Beach getting toheroa and cooking them on the beach. Sometimes we'd all go fishing and feed the whole neighbourhood with our catch. The kids didn't talk Maori. They'd been told to forget about it, and that it wasn't going to be of any use to them. Their parents were trying to integrate them and show them how to be Pakeha."

Alannah did well at school until "the hormones set in" when she was 15, and an interest in boys overtook schoolwork. A rather wild adolescence followed but, as she says, she was good at keeping out of trouble though she often came near. "My mother always said I was born wanting to run away. When I was four, a tatty old circus came and set up on the field at the bottom of the road and I packed my bag and tried to hide in the back of the pony wagon. I didn't get far because my older brother found me and dragged me back home."

Alannah had an English 80-year-old grandmother whose influence became an integral part of her character. "I spent a lot of time with her as

Alannah with her two brothers, Jimmy and Phil

a child. She was constantly feeding me fantastic stories of London and pea-soup fogs and attics full of treasures and cobbled streets and dancing girls. It was in one of her great dusty volumes of the *Encyclopedia Britannica* that I first set eyes on a colour plate entitled 'The Hanging Gardens of Babylon' and I clearly remember just wanting to

43

go there as soon as I could.

"From then on, whenever anyone asked me what I wanted to be when I grew up, I'd just say 'a gypsy'. The world outside New Zealand seemed so much more exciting. My grandmother used to talk about England being home – and she had left there in 1916! She said she could never go back. For me, when I came to England there was a feeling of touching her roots, as well as for myself. She was a great story-teller and she taught me to write and never let the truth get in the way of a good story. She said 'Go out there and see what's going on.' "

At the age of 15 Alannah read Germaine Greer's *The Female Eunuch* on her own in her bedroom. "I thought 'Oh my God! This is the politics of being a girl.' And there was this strange dichotomy of having a mother who would say, 'Go and have a career,' and on the other hand would say, 'I can't afford to put you through university because you are only going to get married anyway, and have babies.' I really loved those women I was raised by, but I didn't want to be like them and have babies at 18 and stay at home. My mother was a very working-class woman and also a feminist and a socialist. She fed me a lot of politics. I was the youngest daughter. I had three older brothers and an older sister, and they had all got pregnant – or someone pregnant – at 18. I think I was my mother's last hope.

"She was an extraordinary woman. We had a state house, and she had a huge vegetable garden because she couldn't afford to buy food. We had chickens which we weren't allowed to name because in the end their heads would be chopped off and we'd be eating them. We often had rabbits and goats, and I even remember a pukeko stew – very stringy. There were lots of children in the street, and often food would be swapped. I was raised thinking that this was normal, and with Maori whanau as neighbours there was more of a community. Everybody looked after everybody else, and for my mother it was absolutely essential. She would always say to me, 'Alannah, always have your own bank account. Never share your money with a man. You always need to know you can run away.' I've always had a separate bank account so I've been able to leave when I want to!" she says, and laughs.

For Alannah growing up in early 1960s' New Zealand, there wasn't a great youth culture, "or if there was, I never found it." Everything exciting, whether it was music or fashion or art, seemed to come from London or New York. "Our education was very English-centred as well. 'Fields of golden daffodils' – there sure weren't any of those in Mt Roskill! I never had a sense of myself as a New Zealander.

"When I was in my early teens I used to dress in my grandmother's clothes and wander around Mt Roskill in these huge hats and long granny coats and you could be sure there was always someone who would come up to me and say, 'Who do you think you are?' People were so nosey and so judgmental. It was that horrible culture, then, of peering through the venetian blinds at the street wedding to check if the bride was wearing white or off-white. Any performance or whatever was called 'showing off'. I felt I was in the wrong place, and needed to go somewhere else. My whole youth just felt like a transit lounge. I felt displaced, not part of my peers, and not part of my family, either."

When Alannah left school she worked as a radio journalist in Wellington for a while and then met an English boy she fell in love with. He wanted to return home, so Alannah decided the time was right to go exploring and left with him. "We arrived in England in 1977 just as punk was exploding. It really was an incredibly exciting time. I used to hang out in the local laundrette, waiting for punks to come in so I could talk to them, and that's the way I met my girlfriend Traci. I formed my first band with her. We called it the Unfuckables." The boy she went to England with wasn't as interested in the music scene as she was, and left one night via the bedroom window. "I never saw much of him again."

Three years later Alannah returned home to see her family, "to just touch the ground, really." She remembers feeling the place was rather old-fashioned. "By then I was completely immersed in music and film and the whole London scene, and it seemed as if that city was the centre of the entire universe. I remember standing on the side of the road in Battersea waiting for a bus. I was wearing a huge Chinese hat and a little mini-skirt made from an old cushion cover, and red rubber boots with very pointy toes, and thinking it was so great that no-one came up to me and said, 'So who do you think you are!' It was utter freedom – bliss." Back in Auckland in 1980, she found the youth culture she had been craving still hadn't appeared. For Alannah it was a lonely place to be if you had a lot of ideas and were looking for like-minded people. "I could never find them. I stayed for three months and then fled back to London. I really didn't come back again until I toured with the Thompson Twins in 1986. This time it was absolutely fantastic. I was treated like a homecoming queen, and my Maori family even organised this huge welcome for us at the airport. It was wild and we had a brilliant time. It was some sort of redemption for me, and I guess by then my strangeness was recognised as having a commercial aspect." Indeed she was getting paid a lot of money for showing off, and was praised for doing good work. Finally she had a stamp of approval from 'over there', and everyone was celebrating her instead of calling her a freak.

"There are musicians I know who tell me they went to New Zealand performing in bands in the 1960s, and they'd finish the performance but couldn't hear anyone applauding. Then they realised it was because everybody had gloves on! When I was a little kid, to go downtown you had to dress up in gloves and a hat, like an odd little English family – it never felt right. It was as if we were all wearing clothes that just didn't fit right."

Alannah and her family, husband Tom Bailey (they are now divorced) and two children, Jackson and Indigo, returned to New Zealand to live in 1993. By then she had spent 16 years living and working in London and the US. She had also toured the world, working and performing everywhere from Berlin to LA to Dublin and back again, 10 times over with the Thompson Twins. "I had lived a very fast, crazy, pop star lifestyle with all the trappings. Then in 1988 I had Jackson and I decided to stop touring and instead stayed in London and just worked on studio pieces and videos. Even with a lot of cash it was really hard to raise a child in London away from family, and I was starting to feel disconnected from the way I was brought up. When I had Indigo in 1993, I decided it was time to move back to New Zealand to raise my babes. I wanted them to have a proper connection with the land I knew and the people I loved."

Moving from inner-city London to the bush by the sea in Matakana north of Auckland was rather a shock to the system, something she hadn't prepared herself for. "I felt a foreigner in my own country. I had forgotten

Alannah back in New Zealand, 1993

how right-wing some small town communities can be, how suspicious of new people, and just how much it rained and how much mud there was everywhere when you lived in the bush. On the other hand I had also forgotten how generous and funny some people are, and how much I loved the green sea and stillness and the great smell of damp earth in the bush. We lasted there three years and missed electricity so much that we moved back to Auckland." In 2004 she returned to London with the children.

Throughout all the years of traveling and living overseas Alannah says she still feels very much a New Zealander. Nonetheless as she is very committed to her London life her allegiances can be sometimes be split. "On good days I have two countries, and on bad days I'm torn," she says. "When I was younger and had left New Zealand I was embarrassed about coming from New Zealand because all people knew about it then was that there were lots of sheep there. I was looking for my own identity, and didn't think it had anything to do with where I came from. It really wasn't until I had children and went back and lived in New Zealand for those 10 years that I got a sense of my self and my place as a New Zealander. Now when I go back to Auckland I walk the streets my mother and grandmother walked, and I feel entirely comfortable there. There is nowhere else in the world that I feel like that. In New Zealand I feel I have turangawaewae – I have a place of cultural entitlement, and I can speak my mind. Even though I have lived in London a long time I don't think I would ever feel as though

I have a right to speak out, not really. For example, I could never start a movement here like Mothers Against Genetic Engineering in Food and the Environment – because I don't have the same passion for this English land as I do for New Zealand.

"I've just moved into a little Victorian house in London and the first thing we did was knock all the walls down. We planted our bush garden and put up big glass windows and invited all the neighbours round. I think a lot of my English friends find that quite shocking. We create the whanau wherever we go. I function much better in a New Zealand way. It's a cultural socialism and I think why New Zealand is looking so good at present is because people have embraced that. In the garden we've got punga, and cabbages all mixed up with English roses."

Alannah's two children were born in London, but having lived in New Zealand in their formative years they consider themselves very much New Zealanders – although at times it can be rather bewildering. "The kids went to school and they were confused about what they were doing, and I said, 'We don't have to do it that way. We're New Zealanders. Just tell them we do it a different way.' We try not to be drawn into the compartmentalised lifestyles that the English have. My children's father is English so they have a New Zealand/English thing, same as I do. They've got two passports, two nationalities, they can choose where they want to live," she says proudly. "When I was first here in the late '70s I was squatting. I had no money and was living in really dire circumstances, but there was always this sort of paradise on the other side of the world that I and the other New Zealanders I knew could always go back to.

"New Zealand is just so rich. We have this incredible land and a huge amount of space. We have a new country with a lot of energy, and we have a really expansive society that holds a lot of promise. I took the children back for three weeks over Christmas, and we were all shocked at how everything is so rich and lush. It's an incredibly comfortable lifestyle. English culture often feels somewhat compartmentalised. For the most part people here live very close to each other in houses divided into small rooms, and everything is done separately in separate nuclear families. There rarely seems to be any great sense of community. I think what Maori brought to the European way of life is a more expansive way of

Alannah Currie

living. The family is not just a nuclear family. It is whanau."

For Alannah there is a downside, however. If you criticise, it can cause problems. In New Zealand so many people are related, and you can be accused of 'having a go' at someone's family. "You might know the third cousin of the third cousin, so it's personal. My kids were talking about violence in London the other day. My teenage son says when somebody mugs you in Auckland it's a personal affront, because you always know somebody who knows somebody, so it feels as if the violence is against the whole community. Here's it's just some random idiot, and it's not personal. I remember one of our guitars got stolen from our house in

Auckland, and the next thing we get a phone call from the guy in the guitar shop up the road. When the thief tried to trade it in, somebody realised it was one of ours and it got back to us. That would never happen in London."

When asked why she went back to London this last time, Alannah says it was the same as the first time. "I was looking for adventure." She also fell in love with an Englishman – an added reason for returning, and on top of that there is always her work. "I work really well in London, possibly because I can be totally anonymous here. I can nurture my work and experiment a lot. If I chose to live in New Zealand now I'm sure I'd have a very comfortable easy lifestyle – but I'm not ready to be comfortable yet. I still have lots of things to do."

Now working as an artist, she says she has become fascinated with chairs, and is part of an underground movement in London called the Arm Chair Destructivists. They recently took an armchair down to Beachy Head on England's south coast and threw it off the cliff. "We filmed it, and took the broken body of the chair and rebuilt it in a distorted manner. We showed all the finished work in a gallery in the West End and it got a good reaction. There's a fantastic underground art movement here that I've become involved in, and I really enjoy working with these artists.

"I do try to keep in touch with what's happening in Auckland's art scene. For such a small country, there is some brilliant work being done. But it sometimes seems that New Zealand art just feeds itself and you rarely see it shown anywhere else. I wish there was more of an exchange of art between the world and New Zealand. New Zealand art is often culturally referential, and it seems as if it's reached the level where there are enough people to buy it and enough people to make it, and there is some fantastic stuff there. Most of the time, though, it never sees the light of day outside of that, and from my perspective I feel it never gets judged against other art in the world, and that's a shame. Sometimes it seems as if it didn't have a koru in the corner then no-one wants to know about it. I've felt my work would have nothing at all to do with any of that.

"Escape is not so easy! The first chair I made here was one I imagined my grandmother had made when she traveled from London to New

Zealand. It was stuffed with seaweed and horsehair and scraps of calico covered in Katherine Mansfield poems. And it was covered in pieces of fabric which could have been her ball gowns, and canvas from her lean-to, and on the arm I drew a map of New Zealand. It was utterly a New Zealand chair, and my friends just laughed at me and said, 'Oh yeah, you can't get away from it.'

"It doesn't matter what I do, it just comes out. It's exciting; it's a culture that's not contained. I just keep coming back to that word 'expansive'. New Zealanders are very generous-spirited and I'm very glad that my children and I are New Zealanders. I watch them and I think you've got that nice New Zealand thing – keep it going! It doesn't matter whether I live in London or New York. It would still come out the same way."

MICHAEL 5 CAMPBELL

MICHAEL CAMPBELL IS VERY GRATEFUL FOR HIS GOLFING LIFESTYLE, BUT WHAT HE regrets is the distance from his Maoritanga. Not that he's complaining. But in the back of his mind is a constant image of himself relaxing with his whanau – sitting out the back of his parents' home in Wellington, maybe a beer in his hand, listening to the easy banter of his beloved language filling the air. When he's ready to tee off, that image is always with him.

Michael's early influences were his golfing mentors and a very large whanau. He proudly points out there were many advantages in being involved in a "gentleman's sport" in the early '70s. Along with those closest to him, golfing taught him etiquette and how to take things in his stride. Indeed, even as a child as young as five, he became aware of the advantage of thinking positively.

"When I was small we fell on hard times and moved from Hawera to Wellington. We moved from a great, laid-back country lifestyle in Taranaki to a state house in Porirua East. But I soon realised that this could be a motivational time for me. I made the best of it. I was very lucky to be surrounded by a lot of love when I was growing up. I've got one sister and 65 first cousins. It was wonderful when all the whanau gathered together at Christmas and Easter. There would be hundreds and hundreds of people. At one stage, I had over 40 aunties and uncles."

Michael was only 10 when he began playing golf after caddying for his dad, Tom, at the Titahi Bay Golf Club. "I told nobody I was playing golf, or only my mum and dad, but none of my friends. Oh no, I didn't tell anybody until I was 16. Why? If I were found out, I would have been ousted from my circle of friends for sure. Golf back in the late '70s and early '80s wasn't the game to play. There were only about five juniors playing at Titahi Bay then. Now there are about 30. On TV recently I saw someone playing for New Zealand who was only about 25. It used to be all guys with grey hair and fat bellies. I remember one day, Mana College in Porirua decided to have a golf day. I was 15 then and I was playing off something like a five handicap, so I volunteered to go and some of my mates volunteered too. By then I had been playing for about eight years and I started smashing those balls. I think they were pretty surprised! Now all my mates play golf, and they all wish they had taken it up at the age of 10, like I did.

"I think the reason I survived growing up in such a rough area was because I just saw nothing else for me but golf. When I was about 17

Michael with whanau, front left

Michael Campbell, junior champion, 12 years old

I lost my direction a bit. I began to feel I should experience something else. When you're surrounded by people a lot older than you, like I was, you grow up very quickly. So I started hanging out with my friends more in the weekends, and I went off the rails a little bit. I stopped practising and started going out to some pretty rough parties. It didn't last too long. I tried it and I didn't like it. I thought, 'This isn't for me. I want to play golf.'"

Michael continues to live with a positive mindset, and firmly believes he needs to be learning more as he gets older. "When you have success people want to know how you did it, and how you got there. I like to compare notes. I believe you should always be asking questions. It's something I'm always telling kids. I ask Tiger or Vijay Singh questions all the time, and I'm the same with business people I meet."

But his success has come at a price. With the vast amount of travelling Michael has done over the last 20 years, and the infrequent visits home, he admits he's lost touch with his language. "Speaking Maori was definitely encouraged throughout my childhood. All my cousins my age speak it quite well but, unfortunately, I don't. I am a Maori New Zealander but I spend so much time away that I lose track of it. It's my own choice, of course. I'm not blaming anybody, but what I'm saying is that you have to make sacrifices. If I were at home a lot, I'd be speaking Maori. When I've been at home, there have been occasions when I've told my mum and dad, and aunties and uncles, to speak to me in Maori, just so I can learn. I really enjoy this.

"Speaking Maori wasn't encouraged at primary school, although at college there was an option to take it up. I think for some time our language was suppressed. But fortunately, I went to school at a time when there was a language revival – the language was acceptable again. I don't feel resentment or anger. I'm not the kind of person who dwells on the past.

"I've just read the *History of New Zealand* with the explanation about how we came to New Zealand in five canoes, and how we met and ate the Moriori. You see, with history, there are always going to be conflicting stories unless you were there yourself. With the Treaty, most Maori feel we were hard done by with the exchange of blankets for rifles. Unfortunately those people who participated sowed the seeds back then, and now people are trying to make it right. The most important thing is for the European and Maori to live in harmony because it's a very small country. When I play golf I represent New Zealand – not only Maori. I represent all Kiwis."

Michael is very proud of his culture and is on a mission to "expose it to the world". With all the travelling he does, and being constantly in the public eye, he is in a position to reach a wide range of people and talk to them about Maoridom. "I've got my own clothing line, and most of it bears motifs that mean something to me. I've been very fortunate to be able to do this," he says. "It's all about exposure. When Americans come across the silver fern, they often say, 'Oh, that's the All Blacks.' I think the silver fern has definitely become an iconic symbol of New Zealand, more so than the kiwi."

Every time he returns to New Zealand he sees it through different eyes, and because of his fame he finds people see him differently. "Because of this I feel I don't get the true picture of how people feel about the interaction between Maori and Pakeha. There are times when people don't recognise me — and this can be anywhere in world — and I find it's kind of nice when people treat me normally. In fact, it can be quite funny, but then all of a sudden the penny drops and their whole demeanour changes, and I've lost it. It's the nature of the beast, I guess. At first, when I became famous, it was weird, to have people admire me, watch everything I do, and know that everything they were reading in the newspapers they thought was a true reflection of me. Sometimes I make mistakes, but now I use this recognition as a tool to raise awareness and money back home. It's great to be able to help young people from disadvantaged backgrounds to fulfil their dreams.

"It's crazy when I go back to New Zealand. I'm only able to do a trip about twice a year, and I try and squeeze so much into that time as well as trying to see my whanau and my mates from school. By now it's almost impossible. I made my bed and I've got to sleep in it, I guess, and I'm certainly not complaining. The main thing is it's wonderful to be home, and I do miss New Zealand a lot. I miss the culture. I miss the 'Kiwiness'. People at home are very relaxed. I'm so used to the fast lane now and after a week in New Zealand I'm saying, 'Come on, let's do something!' It's good for me to unwind but I can't really relax altogether back home because I'm in demand for public appearances – and I'm glad to do this for a good cause. But there always has to be an hour or two when I will do nothing. It's very important to me.

"People around me overseas are too shy to say anything critical about New Zealanders. Really, I'm serious! Although I do get the occasional

Michael with his sons Thomas and Jordan

sheep joke. In the golfing world you've got to be very thick-skinned. If you react to what people say you won't last too long out there. Americans are so intrigued because all the clothes I wear have Maori designs on them, and they want to find out who I am and what the designs mean. I find it's a little project to educate them, and they go, 'Oh really, do you guys wear those grass skirts?' I say, 'Are you kidding?' But they are serious. It's bizarre."

With Michael's two children being schooled in England and Australia, they have little contact with their father's culture. "It's very hard because I don't know much myself anymore, but I always try to teach them through books. When we're at home, Mum and Dad try to teach them Maoritanga, but it's very difficult. We lead such transient lives because I play golf in so many countries. One important thing I've taught them is to learn from the world." He does his best to surround himself with as many reminders of home as possible. "All through both my houses I've got Kiwi artefacts everywhere. I've even got four ponga trees in the garden of our England home." His Australian wife, Julie, empathises with Michael's culture. "Although, when New Zealand play against Australia in sport, the house is very silent!" Then he laughs.

He says people don't see how hard he works. All they see is the travelling to all the beautiful places, and the generous prizes. "A friend of mine came over to England for a week and saw what I did. When he left he said, 'You can have your life, bro.' It's all the fitness and training, and it's also about time management. Sometimes that can be very difficult, but I've learnt to say no to some people. Every day I have hour-long talks with my managers. We discuss proposals for me to be an ambassador for this and that, and then flying somewhere for some speech. I just can't do it all. But I'm trying to spread myself out and at the same time be here for my kids. One thing Greg Norman told me was that the only regret he had in his career was a five-year gap where he missed seeing his kids growing up. Jack Nicklaus told me he never spends more than two weeks away from his family. So just listening to these legends of golf has taught me a lot. I think the most important thing is to be your own advisor. People tell you their opinions, and it's a matter of filtering some of it out and keeping the rest for yourself.

Michael receiving the award of CNZM

"I've been to a lot of dinners and functions around the world and people might say to me, 'Oh, that's a really Kiwi thing to say,' and I can't remember what I actually said! But there really are differences between Kiwis and the rest of the world. And it's not just the All Blacks and the haka and the culture. And the sheep." And he laughs again.

People in the mostly Maori environment were "pretty placid" when he was growing up but he thinks that in the last 20 years many have become aggressive. "That aggression in *Once Were Warriors* was all there because alcohol was involved. Alcohol and Pacific Islanders do not go together. Back in the old days all we had were spears for hunting moa. We ran around, we were athletes, and we were fit and strong. When the Europeans arrived, they gave us guns and sugar. Sugar and alcohol don't go together. You end up with fat people with a huge problem. Most Maori people who are not exercising are overweight because they have been exposed to Western society.

"My 'drug' of choice is being the best I can possibly be in what I'm doing, and if possible, being the best in the world. That's what gets me up in the morning. That's what gets me going to the gym to do an hour on the bike and go to a spin class. I have to ask myself why I am doing this. But I know it's because it's going to make me stronger! Its discipline, which is something I learnt from going to school. 'Michael, time to get up for school,' Mum said that to me every morning for 12 years. It was a pain, but really it was routine and it was a discipline. That stood me in good stead, but some people rebelled because it was too regimented for them.

"When I stand on that first tee, thinking I'd rather be at home cooking dinner, then it'll be time to chuck it in. But right now the fire is burning inside me and I know I have another good seven years to play this game, and play as hard as I can.

"People's personalities come out on the golf course. Some people are very analytical and you can see this develop as they play. The biggest enemy is yourself. If you convince yourself you are good enough, then you will perform. People around you will say that you're good, but the most

The Michael Campbell the world sees

powerful thought processes are your own. You have a dozen thoughts a day so you have to make sure that every one of them is positive so that every thought is good. There are certain frustrations that can set in, but I'm pretty calm most of the time out there. It's a bad image if you start throwing things around. It's all about etiquette. It's a different game from other games and you walk around in pristine conditions, so it's a different kind of environment from, say, a rugby game.

"Luck comes into it, but I believe you make your own luck in golf, and life. I'm a big believer that what you put out is equal to what you get back. I can hit a tee shot and make sure it goes through the trees and gets a good bounce, and if I try to will the ball to go in the right direction, it might do it.

"I believe every thought has a frequency. If we send out good thoughts to a friend or our mum and dad, in time it will make itself be felt. I practised this the weekend of the US Open in 2005. I felt in total control. I was controlling more things than my golf game. It was a lovely feeling."

He is heartened by the sight of more Maori playing sports. Seeing the Maori players in the Black Caps is an example of how far things have come. "I was back home recently and I went to a golf academy and most of the students there were Maori kids about 13 or 14 years of age, and I thought that was great."

As a kid he often asked himself why there weren't any professional Maori golfers on tour. "I set up the Michael Campbell Foundation to try to make a difference. I wanted to help show kids, not just Maori kids, that there were more sports besides the usual rugby and rugby league." It's one of his great joys that he thinks his foundation is making a difference.

PAULA 6 MORRIS

PAULA MORRIS LIVES IN NEW ORLEANS WHERE SHE IS ASSISTANT PROFESSOR OF English at Tulane University. As a writer who lives in America yet more often than not writes novels and stories set in New Zealand, she draws on her West Auckland spirit and the images in her mind of a country she loves and perpetually misses.

But she doesn't feel pressure – or the need – to set her work in the South Pacific. "I don't think I have to prove, through my work, that I'm still loyal to New Zealand," she says. "Writers should write what they like to write, just as painters should paint what they like to paint. Everybody should be free to make whatever art they want. Some of it may fit into the big picture of creating a national literature, and some may not."

Living in America does not in any way cloud her view of her homeland. She may even be a more fervent Kiwi now, than before she left the country. Speaking from New Orleans, she stresses the conflict of wanting a writer's freedom, but at the same time wanting to be perceived as a New Zealand writer.

"When I think of my childhood, I suppose it was quite free in many ways. It didn't have the anxieties and pressures that many of my friends who were brought up overseas experienced. I guess it was all that barefoot, open, laid-back lifestyle we had. A lot of people would envy that kind of childhood. When I tell people over here that it wasn't really compulsory to wear shoes to primary school, they are quite horrified.

"I went to Rutherford High School where I had excellent teachers. I've been patronised about it many times by some Aucklanders abroad, usually people who went to private schools. At one stage I had a pretty high-powered career in New York in the record industry, and having these people turn up and patronise me about my high school when I had my PhD and was a vice-president of my company, was a bit much. How far do you have to go, and how old do you have to be, to escape that kind of thing? I'm sure if I turned up at the North Pole, there would be somebody there saying, 'You went to Rutherford? Oh!'

"This idea that there was some disadvantage to going to a state school never entered my head, and it's so bogus to hear it from fellow New Zealanders. We were brought up to believe that you made your own fortune in life, and, as my mother used to say – which drove us crazy at the time – 'The world is your oyster'."

Paula's mother is English, and she met and married Paula's father, who is part-Maori, in England. She would never have chosen to come to New Zealand if she hadn't met him, Paula says. Arriving in 1964 in New Zealand, after living in London, Paris and Luxembourg, Paula's mother had to be a brave woman, she thinks. Her father was doing the usual OE in Europe when they met – like going to bullfights in Spain and acting as an extra in a movie. "He actually appeared in *Cleopatra*, but we've never been able to pick him out! He had been an apprentice at the *New Zealand Herald* before going overseas and they kept his job open for years while he was away – those were the days." After living with Paula's grandparents in Ponsonby, they settled in Te Atatu South, a growing suburb in West Auckland, in 1966.

"Life must have been pretty different for my mother, adjusting from life in the bustling cities of Europe to quiet suburbia in Auckland. My father's family were very welcoming to her. My mother was very close to her mother-in-law, but her family and my father's family could not be more different. It was only when my English grandmother came out that we realised we came from two completely different families. When my English grandmother came out for a visit she would sit only in a hard-backed chair, whereas after a Sunday lunch my Maori grandmother would lie on the floor quite happily and fall asleep.

"Race or ethnicity was never an issue in the neighbourhood I grew up in. Half-caste is a term I never heard, and would never use. We had lots of ethnicities and nationalities out West – Dutch, Croatian, Lebanese, Maori, Polynesian. And many of my classmates had at least one British parent, like me. Some people question me quite aggressively – 'Did you join the Maori club at school?' or 'Do you speak fluent Maori?' – and then declare whether I'm Maori or not, as though it's something they can pronounce on. I hate other people thinking they can decide this for me. I know who I am."

Paula remembers being teased at primary school after she told a teacher about her Maori lineage. "I was telling a teacher who had come out from England that my great-grandmother was the daughter of a chief, and an important person in our family, and the teacher, who was quite fond of me, called me her little Maori princess. Some of the kids teased me endlessly about this – not about being Maori, but for daring to be a princess!

"When I went to the University of Auckland and started hanging out with kids from other schools and neighbourhoods, it was the first time

Paula with her grandmother and mother

I'd really thought about being perceived as 'other' or having to define my allegiances. I would hang out with all these kids from expensive, private, largely white schools and they would say things like, 'There aren't any full-blooded Maori any more.' I'd get really annoyed and tell them my grandmother was, even though this, admittedly, wasn't really true. But that kind of comment – which you still hear from some people today, unfortunately – is really about the fear of the resurgence in Maori culture, as well as profound disrespect. The implication is that Maori are getting above their station and there aren't any full-blooded ones anyway – so why take their claims seriously? I suppose that was the beginning of my political consciousness, when I realised it was fine for many people if Europeans inherited land, but not if Maori did.

"It's like people saying the Queen of England is not entitled to be Queen, because she has German blood. The fact that my father married somebody from England doesn't mean I can't trace my ancestry back and belong to a marae and be part of a family. As one of my cousins says, being Maori is about kinship, not about the colour of your skin. It's a question of heritage, of inheritance – and I loathe the idea that you can be turfed out of your own heritage. When my father dies, my siblings and I will inherit his land, just as he inherited it from his mother who inherited it from her father, and so on, back to Chief Te Kiri. I don't see why this is ok for the royal family yet not acceptable for Maori."

Paula left New Zealand in 1985, just after she turned 20, to do post-graduate studies in English and Women's Studies at the University of York in England. After she finished her doctorate she moved to London, working at the BBC and then in the record industry. In 1994 she moved to New York to work in marketing for another record company – "When someone offers you a job in New York, you don't really say no." She didn't get to live back in New Zealand until 2001 when she and her American husband, Tom Moody, spent the year in Wellington. There she completed Bill Manhire's MA in creative writing at Victoria University, and wrote her first novel, *Queen of Beauty*. In 2002 Paula and Tom returned to the US, heading to the famed Iowa Writers' Workshop, where Paula had been awarded a Schaeffer fellowship. After she graduated with an MFA in 2004, they moved again, this time to New Orleans: Paula is now a faculty member at Tulane University, teaching creative writing. "There are very few similar jobs in New Zealand. Unfortunately, it's a small place and, in some areas, there are fewer opportunities than elsewhere. But I go back to New Zealand to visit as often as possible. Last year I was home three times; and in 2005 I spent six weeks in Auckland after evacuating for Hurricane Katrina. It was our second hurricane there, and our second evacuation. I was starting to wonder if we were being punished for moving to New Orleans."

Paula graduating from university in 1985

In spite of living in the US for more than a decade, Paula doesn't see herself as American in any way. "I'm a New Zealander. I'm not one of these people who say they've left their country behind. Nobody here thinks I'm an American, not simply because of my accent, or because I eat different foods from them, especially at Christmas. When I was growing up I saw the same films and a lot of the same television that people my age saw in America, but it was a different experience for me. Because of our peculiar history and geography and cultural heritage, New Zealanders have a different way of viewing the world.

"I absolutely feel that New Zealanders are just as patriotic as the Americans. We just don't rally around the flag so much, and we don't have a national holiday we can agree on. Tom and I were at a Mardi Gras parade recently, where there were lots of marching bands playing, and we were standing near some quite drunk people. They were shouting 'USA! USA!' I can't imagine being in New Zealand and having the equivalent happening. I just don't think that's us. But it doesn't mean we don't feel it. We are a pretty self-deprecating nation, and perhaps that's why Waitangi Day is often fraught. It's not just accepted – we don't all go out and light fireworks, and buy into a big sunny national myth. I think the controversy that has dogged Waitangi Day in the past reflects a nation that's still coming to terms with its own history."

Paula wonders if the increasing interest in local historical fiction is because people are trying to make sense of the past and trying to work out who they are. "Look at the huge success of Michael King's *History of New Zealand*. By October 2007, sales had reached 230,000 in the basic paperback editions. That kind of figure would be extraordinary even for a historical book in America. I think people really want to know about, and understand, our history. I'm really appalled here in the US when I come across students who know very little about American history. I think it's crucial to understand why things are the way they are. In the 6th form, when I did an incredibly interesting New Zealand history class covering the Land Wars, it made me realise all these things about my country that I didn't really understand before. Maybe the growing interest in our own history reflects a growing awareness of what New Zealand is. Maybe in the past it was seen as just a colonial outpost, easily understood and defined, easily dismissed." Our unique Maori-Pakeha heritage, Paula believes, "is the thing that distinguishes New Zealand from the rest of the world. I love that it's a vital part of New Zealand."

While she thinks some New Zealanders can be "quite narrow-minded", Paula thinks most are tolerant and welcoming. She jokes that "socialism is one of our fine traditions" and suggests that social change "always feels possible, perhaps because we don't have centuries of tradition to overcome. We don't have vast ruling classes who have been protecting their own vested interest for centuries. Because I don't keep in close enough touch with New Zealand politics when I'm away, I don't vote when I'm overseas. In fact, I don't really believe in absentee voting. I don't feel I should vote unless I'm back and very much engaged in what's going on."

Although she does admit to checking out New Zealand newspaper websites everyday to keep in touch with what's happening at home, she's not too sure if this helps her ongoing homesickness. "A friend visited us here recently and said, 'My God, what have you been doing all these years? Your house is so full of New Zealand things!' I think she thought it rather strange. Every time I return from home I've brought more paintings and books. I think if I lived in New Zealand my house would be the same. I like to be surrounded by things from home. In our office at the back of the house I have lots of New Zealand pictures, and while I was writing my last book, *Hibiscus Coast*, which is set in New Zealand, I had maps covering the walls. When I needed the characters to drive from Mt Wellington to the Domain, I'd call up my father to ask how they would get there – he knows every road in Auckland – because I had to have it clear in my head. Part of that novel was set down by Princes Wharf, so on a visit home I rushed around taking photos. In the novel, I had to change some of it to suit my purposes, but I needed to get a feeling of the real place. I like to have photos around me to remind myself of things like the light – that peculiar sharp light at home. And also, New Zealand readers will always tell me when I've made a mistake!"

She pauses to think, and laughs. "When I was in England people relentlessly criticised my New Zealand accent. Then I went home and I was criticised for sounding English. These days, living in the US, it's all down to the choice of words. I'm generally quite good at switching, so I might say 'elevator' here and 'lift' to a New Zealander, but if I don't correct myself, someone else will. It can be a bit tiring. With emails I'm always changing the spelling from American to English when writing home.

"I warn people when I hear they're going to New Zealand for a visit, because I often think Americans are very deluded about it. They think it's paradise and they can just wander around anywhere and leave their keys dangling in the car door. My students considering a trip to New Zealand think they can hitchhike and wander around with no shoes on and not get into trouble. They might be ok, but, as we know, there are tourists who get robbed and murdered. It's hard to persuade them that everywhere has a dark side, and that New Zealand has many of the same contemporary social problems as bigger countries. When I lived in Iowa City one of the things I liked about it was that I could walk around at night without being afraid, because it was the first place I'd ever lived in my life where

I felt like that. People say to me, surely in New Zealand you can do that? But would I walk down darkened streets in Auckland without thinking there could be anything threatening me? Absolutely not! I don't think any New Zealander would ever think it was a completely safe place, however patriotic they may be.

"People see *Lord of The Rings* and they think that's what New Zealand looks like, and I say, 'Mmm ... well, yes and no.' We're not as docile and well-mannered as we seem, and there's an undercurrent of depression –maybe it's aggression, maybe it's yearning, maybe it's frustration. The beauty of our landscape that gets promoted overseas and the cheery hospitality of New Zealanders – which is true – aren't the whole story. We're not quite as simple a country as our tourist campaigns suggest."

Paula admits, however, that "the Tourist Board campaign is clearly very effective. When I see the ads here, I think 'Oh gosh, New Zealand *is* lovely'. But at the same time it's not simply a placid, characterless film-set. Like many countries, we have people who feel discontent and people who feel very isolated and hopeless. When I was home last year on a tour with five other writers, we visited a great school in Northland where the kids did a powhiri for us, and gave moving and articulate speeches. But a lot of their parents are unemployed, and there is very little for them there. To have a future, they'll have to move away."

When her third novel, *Trendy But Casual* – an all-American story – was recently published in New Zealand, Paula says she was 'waiting for the stones to rain down' because of the New York city setting. "I can imagine there is a certain school of thought that believes New Zealand authors who set books in other countries want to commodify our literature, sell in countries other than New Zealand and create a viable career for themselves, instead of helping construct a national literature. I think this happens with young and small countries, or perhaps countries in the process of building a post-colonial identity and writing their own histories. I read an interview with a Mexican writer who was asked, 'If you're not setting your books in Mexico, are you really a Mexican writer?'

"I think anyone who's been under the colonial thumb at some point,

Paula Morris

where people are more conscious of having their own history, it becomes an issue. There isn't the same pressure for an American or English writer – if you're an English writer you can set your novel in Russia and no one will say a thing. Certainly we don't put the same heavy burden on our pop stars, and if a New Zealand athlete went to train in America and did really well, New Zealanders would be delighted. With literature it's a little different, because we're telling our country's stories. But I think my only real responsibility is to avoid stereotypes, and I certainly feel a personal responsibility to make my books entertaining. Sometimes I think New Zealand literature gets a bad rap from other New Zealanders, who say they read a New Zealand novel once and didn't like it, so they're not reading any others. Or they characterise all New Zealand novels as too gloomy, stark and depressing.

"I really like writing about Auckland now and the way it changes, and I suppose I do feel a responsibility to be true to the place in a way. But it's always going to be my take on it. I don't feel I should write a book because it is a book that is 'needed'. I've argued before that New Zealand writers should be free to write about whatever they want without people saying they should be contributing to the national literature in some proscribed way. I feel that very strongly. It takes such a long time to write a book that you really have to be into your subject matter. If you're going to spend two or three years on something, you have to feel very passionate about it personally, rather than worrying if it's serving the good of the nation. My American agent would love it if I wrote only American books, but I think I should do whatever it is that I want to do, and accept the fact that the book in question will be of interest or sell only in some places."

At high school in the 1970s and early 1980s, Paula says they "didn't read a lot of New Zealand literature – mainly Katherine Mansfield and Frank Sargeson, both of whom felt quite remote from me. It was only when we saw a film of one of Witi Ihimaera's short stories that I realised stories could be set in contemporary Auckland.

"In terms of being a Maori writer, I know that some people are quite happy to embrace me into the fold. Witi, for instance, has been extremely supportive, and recently asked me for a short story for an anthology he's editing of Maori writing. Patricia Grace, another Maori writer I admire, has been very kind. But I have noticed that some critics who talk about Maori writing don't include me, perhaps because my Maori characters live in the city and because many of them are middle-class. They don't fit the stereotype. My settings and my subject matter aren't exactly *Once Were Warriors*, so to people who have a narrow view of Maori experience, it seems as though it's not really Maori writing."

That very important part of Paula's life, Maoritanga, is sometimes hard to explain to her American friends. When a story she set in Auckland was discussed at a the Iowa Writers' Workshop, a classmate asked her where the Maori live – expecting to hear 'on a reservation'. This doesn't deter her from writing about New Zealand, even though she's far from home. "It's absolutely who I am, and it's part of my family history and what I'm really proud of. The big 19th century novel I'm working on at present is based on a short story I wrote which itself is based on an oral history I found written by one of my ancestors, Paratene Te Manu. His life spanned the 19th century, from fighting with Hongi Hika during the Musket Wars to visiting Queen Victoria in the 1860s to being evicted from Little Barrier Island, along with my great-grandparents, in the 1890s.

"To me, being Maori is about embracing your cultural inheritance and being connected. Someone has said to me that they thought much of my writing was about race and nationhood, and in that sense very profoundly New Zealand. It's always really strange when someone defines your work for you, but I guess that is a very important current in my writing. I'm interested in how New Zealand became a country and how it is continually changing and becoming a different place. Even if I live in America for the rest of my life – God help me! – I would still be a New Zealander because I don't think you can escape who you are, even if you want to. And because I believe who you are is formed, to a large extent, by the place where you grow up. I'm ashamed to say I can't really imagine writing a novel set on the North Shore, for example, even though I've set a short story there. The part of New Zealand that has any real significance for me is West Auckland. That's close enough to home for me."

TEDDY TAHU RHODES

FROM HIS NAME YOU WOULD EXPECT TEDDY TAHU RHODES TO BE MAORI. BUT no. The name of Tahu was the name bestowed on an ancestor, and has been passed down for several generations to Teddy, a name he carries proudly. He sees it as a connection to New Zealand and the Pacific Island culture he feels very much a part of.

Many reviewers wax lyrical over his striking Nordic looks while putting his admirable singing talent to one side. This is a pity, as even his rich speaking voice can carry clearly over a crowded Sydney restaurant, a talent many other celebrities would give their eye teeth for.

Teddy grew up in Christchurch. When he left school, opera singing was way down the list of options. "I don't know why I went into accountancy. Well, I suppose I do. I went to Christ's College and my peers were all off to do law and accounting. As I was useless at the sciences, I didn't contemplate doing anything else but follow in their footsteps. I was enjoying singing, but I never considered doing it for a living. My role model was the college's choir master, Bob Field Dodgson, who encouraged me to join the choir. I remember it was the last day of my school life, and Mum was there at the departing service, and he said to her that one day, if I wanted to, I could make a career out of my singing. I was 18 at the time and it was quite a big thing to hear. Of course I never took it very seriously. He was probably the first person who could see I had something. I still had the chance to get a good grounding through the choir.

"My singing life has two stages. I took singing lessons at university as part of a performance singing course I did with my commerce degree. I was picked out as someone with potential, and when I was 20 I won the Dame Sister Mary Leo Scholarship. After I left university I studied in London at the Guildhall, also on a scholarship and I eventually won the Mobil Song Contest, I had been in it three times running, I think they wanted to get rid of me! When I was 24 I came home, and for the next seven years I did IT and accounting work.

"I still did the odd gig, Canterbury Opera stuck by me and I did a couple of gigs for them, and people such as Chris Doig, Malvina Major, Brian Law and my dear singing teacher Mary Adams Taylor all kept saying 'Come on, you should be doing something with this.' But it would have been a complete change of life for me. I was married and it didn't fit into any of our future plans. Unfortunately when I turned 30 my marriage broke up, and that same year I was offered Marcello in *La Boheme*. Somebody heard me and went back to Australia and said, 'You should hear this guy.' I gave my job up and came across to Australia and then it just went on from there."

Teddy as a boy

While Teddy's opera career developed in America and Europe, he sang in a couple of operas in New Zealand, and from this experience he has found New Zealand offers the young performer a huge amount. "Even when I went to the Guildhall at the age of 23 I had already sung with the NZ Symphony Orchestra. New Zealanders with potential come from such a small pool, but there are some there who are really keen to nurture that talent. Overseas people ask why there are so many good singers coming out of New Zealand. It seems to me they are the ones who have been given encouragement and guidance, and they work pretty hard to get there.

"We have to travel so far to take it further, and I think all singers from New Zealand feel very strongly that they are representing New Zealand. There is a charm about our coming from New Zealand. A few of us are dotted around in opera, and they are all doing wonderfully well. Two of us were in Vienna recently doing *A Streetcar Named Desire*, Simon O'Neill and I. It had a cast of four main roles and two of them were filled by New Zealanders."

Although Teddy spends most of his time performing in some of the most beautiful cities in the world, if it came to buying a piece of land to call home his first choice would be Auckland. "I'm always on the internet looking at the New Zealand market. I romanticise about buying an Auckland property, but it's not practicable at present. I always think I'll go back, as I can't imagine settling somewhere else. I feel more grounded in Auckland than Christchurch, despite the fact I grew up there and I know it inside out. I just love the culture of Auckland. I'm a New Zealander and I want to live at home, but my diary's booked up until 2010. It crosses my mind sometimes to retire. If I've had a crap review I think, oh damn it I'll go home and do something else. I hanker for that life, but I'm sure if I did it now I'd get bored with it. It doesn't matter how beautiful a city is, if you haven't got an affinity with it, or friends there, they are all just big cities and nothing else. I've recently sung in Paris and it's a fantastic city, with a buzz about it, and it's so charming. But I don't know anybody there apart from my colleagues. While you're doing a show in a city you have a purpose for being there. The day the show finishes and everyone leaves, you suddenly feel like a foreigner because your purpose for being there has gone. It might be beautiful, but you're not needed."

Teddy's parents are a mixture of Kiwi and English. They met in England, and his mother, from Kent, worked for the Rhodes family on their estate. The Tahu name was bestowed on a member of his family by the Ngati Tahu tribe several generations back. "I've often wondered whether I'd take it any further, but I do love the name. I had a brother

Teddy competing in the Mobil Song Contest, 1987

called Teddy Tahu who died aged eight from leukaemia. My parents passed the name on to me several years later when I was born. I did a piece in Christchurch a couple of years ago which was based around the Ngati Tahu tribe and looked at the history of both Maori and Pakeha coming to Canterbury. For me it was my history." He does lot of modern opera and thinks new audiences could be brought in. The art form could be expanded and made more relevant to what people do today, and where they came from. "It will be a great shame if opera doesn't go anywhere, and in 200 years' time all we are thinking of is Mozart. If you go to Europe every small town has an opera house, it is part of their culture. However, I don't think in New Zealand the appreciation is any less than it is elsewhere. It's just that our pool is smaller.

"In Auckland if you took away the Auckland Philharmonic and the New Zealand Opera, which probably only a small percentage of the population attend, you would still be taking something very important away from the city. If I got offered more work at home I could spend more time there. The hard thing is it's your job, and you have to sustain yourself, so if you get an offer for an opera in Europe which is three years in advance, you take it. In New Zealand it's difficult for them to plan so far ahead because they don't know what funding they will get. It was only the other day Simon O'Neill and I were talking about ways we could get back to New Zealand to do more work there."

Taking into account the small fan base that opera singers have, as compared with rock singers, it had never crossed Teddy's mind that he's not too well known in New Zealand, even in Australia. "Well, I am with the people who follow opera, but okay, I admit that's about it. You're kind of just famous in your own little world, aren't you? I don't feel I've picked opera especially; I feel it picked me. Ultimately it's not really important because I'm still living the life that I want to live. I don't worry that there are people back home who don't know me. Then again it's always very flattering when people do recognise you, and it can be quite bizarre. I go from job to job travelling around the world and sometimes I pinch myself that I'm performing in, say Paris, but I want to continue that and my main focus is to continue to be good at what I do."

In honour of his name and his affinity with Maori culture Teddy has a Maori tattoo on his upper arm, done in a style seen on some celebrities and many rugby players. "I decided to get it done the day after my 39th birthday. I'd been thinking about it for some time. It's funny because I hardly notice it now, but people recognise it immediately. The other night the wife of one of the other singers, a New Zealander, noticed it while I was on stage. A couple of days later we were all having lunch together and she realised it was still there. She'd thought it was stage make-up.

"I'm not Maori, but I'm a New Zealander, and as I'm travelling the world I felt compelled to have something distinctly of our country and culture. So I went to a Maori guy in Sydney and we designed something that was completely non-tribe-based but distinctly Maori. Maori and Pakeha cultures are entirely different, but the melding of the two is very much New Zealand today. I've been away from the country for a while now, but travelling around the world I think it's wonderful that people see our culture as very much Maori-Pacific Island. They identify me as a Pacific Islander when I say I'm a New Zealander. To water our culture down would be a tragedy. Both the Pakeha and Maori cultures need to be cherished separately and together. I didn't learn Maori at school – I was never given the chance. You can't ignore I'm Pakeha, but to be part of the Maori and Pacific Islander culture is so beautiful. No, I wouldn't have considered a union jack tattoo. I don't feel English in the slightest."

As he travels the world he finds that New Zealand is looked upon as a society to be respected, and MMP is seen as a role model in parliamentary procedures. "Helen Clark is great, and I think we've had some great politicians. David Lange was amazing. I loved his book. I appreciate the diversity of what we have, and it seems your vote is worth something. New Zealand still has a bit of fairness about it. I think it's getting more expensive to live there, which is making it tougher, but when I think of going back I think of that fairness, and the beauty of that bit of land."

Teddy is applauded in the great opera houses of the world, but unlike other major stars he travels solo without any 'people' to reassure him every step of the way. "There've been a number of times I've been in my dressing room about to go on stage in a big house, and it's opening night and I'm there wandering around, and I don't know a single soul. It can feel kind of shallow. Sure, what I'm doing is amazing, it's wow I'm in New York and someone has invited me to stand on the stage at the Met, and to sing! And yeah, the audience out there waiting for the curtain to go up has heard some of the great singers singing it all before. So there is an incredible expectation.

"I have to shake myself out of it, and not think of it that way. I just do what I can at that moment. When I'm finished I go back to my hotel room and sit and drink a glass of wine and watch CNN.

"If people appreciate what I do, and they want me back, then all is well and good. I'm not saying this about every performance, but every now and again in a bad moment, by yourself, there tend to be thoughts of wanting to go home and sit on the veranda of that house I want in Auckland and have a beer. It would be ideal if after every performance I had that to go home to.

"I'm not in the league of Michael Campbell, of having managers around me. He's an identifiable figure, a product of his talent. I think he's awesome. I probably get about only five emails a day, and my agent

Teddy Tahu Rhodes

takes care of most of the bookings. So it's just me and a few suitcases. I flew into Sydney after finishing a seven-week run in Vienna and Munich. In two weeks I've got three gigs to do, rehearsal gigs and TV. Then I'll hit Paris running. I know it's busy, but this is my life. I actually had 10 days free at Christmas, which I hadn't had for a long time and I spent it in Perth with family, walking on the beach and sitting on the veranda. It was great. You feel the benefit, but then you have all this work to do when you come back. I wasn't supposed to have any music with me – I was taking a break from work. I went 10 days without singing, so it was really hard to come back and it took about four days to get my voice back into shape. To do this kind of work I need to be fit and go to the gym every day. It can be hard work, performing."

One of Teddy's favourite moments with any opera is when he gets to rehearse for the first time with the orchestra. "Standing up there when an

80-piece orchestra begins playing, and this beautiful sound wafts up and you sing with it, and together you make this wonderful music ... I can only describe it as an enormous engine behind you, and you are just another cog in that glorious machine. I hear myself sometimes and I think, whoa! It's a privilege, an absolute privilege." As for the groupies. "Yeah, they're there at the stage door. I do have one you could have called a groupie in the beginning, but she's now a good friend. She's German and travels around to hear me sing all over Europe. She's blind and is a big opera fan. I can't imagine what it would be like, sitting there with my eyes closed and listening to it live. Maybe she is hearing more than everyone else in the audience. But isn't that the joy of opera? The music is beautiful, and the singing and the story should take you somewhere else. Perhaps that's where she is going, somewhere where she can see. To hear her talk about it makes me understand the beauty even more. For me, when I'm on that stage performing all I want is the audience to go home happy."

Whenever Teddy returns to Christchurch he is always taken aback by the vast Canterbury landscape. He says that even in his childhood he loved the feeling of space. "I love the green and the smell, it's really different, it's a freshness, and a lack of pace. You know what's really interesting? It's the juxtaposition. If you are standing in Canterbury, for example, there is always something on the horizon. You can see so far to the mountains. We have this space in New Zealand and the horizon is never far away. You can be standing in the middle of America and it's endless, and there is the feeling of it's going on forever. But in New Zealand, even though we have these broad expanses of nature there is an intimacy about it because you can see it – you're not actually that far away from it.

"I used to love helping out on my cousin's farm out of Christchurch in the school holidays. I remember hearing opera on the radio. We'd would be sitting in the farm truck, and he would have the classical music station on, and I'd say, 'Come on, what do you have that on for?' and he would say, 'When you get to my age that's all you'll listen to.' It's not all I listen to, but of course I didn't know the relevance of what he was saying back then. I was out drenching sheep in the rolling paddocks, and that was enough fun for me."

JON STEVENS

For more than half his life, singer Jon Stevens has lived away from New Zealand. No matter. His feelings about his country are the same as the day he left.

"The pull of New Zealand is always there, but I'll never give up wanting to travel because I love adventure. I've been happy to be out in the world and experiencing different cultures. All this has made me understand my own culture even more strongly. I'm part of a really rich heritage. It's in my soul, it never leaves me," he explains. He agrees that many people have to leave New Zealand before they understand and fully appreciate where they've come from.

"I'm a Kiwi through and through. I'm part-Maori and I was brought up with my Maori culture, and the fact that I've spent most of the time since I was 17 years old travelling the world doesn't change what I feel about who I am. If you come to my house you will find Maori art and carvings everywhere, plus some from other indigenous cultures. I'm very big on keeping that a part of my life."

Jon is the youngest of 11 children from what he calls a typical Upper Hutt working-class family, his parents being of mixed descent. His mum was Maori and his dad Scottish. "We didn't have TV or a car or a phone. We were just an ordinary Maori family. My parents worked their butts off so they could feed us. In the early days Maoritanga was frowned on. It wasn't talked about much at all.

"There was no black or white at home when I was growing up, but then as I got older a few racial things came into play, although I never let it be part of my life. You know, I think that's a very Kiwi thing to do. My philosophy is one that is born out of the streets of Upper Hutt and Wellington – I'm nice to everybody until they aren't nice to me. "

His description of his Maori culture is of being both warrior and family-orientated, something he says he's very proud of. "I remember growing up with friends who had babies really young, and instead of adopting them out they would be given to someone in the whanau and they were brought up in the same family. And as weird as some people might think that is for young kids who got into trouble like that, back then it happened pretty often. I've always thought it was great that the babies stayed in the family at least 99 percent of the time.

"I was expelled from school in 1975. I was only 14. Back in those days you got the cane or the strap if you were naughty, or you were perceived to be naughty. Not only was I the youngest in our family but we all went to the same schools. When I got to secondary school I was confronted by a teacher who swore at me and said, 'I can't wait to get rid of you, boy!' He'd had enough of us Stevens kids. It was kind of war from there on in, which eventually led me to leave school.

"I had to get a job. I come from that era where you didn't muck around. I felt I was a man when I was still just a boy. This was in a town where there were a lot of gangs and a lot of violence. I saw things that kids should never see. "

Jon was only 15 when he won a talent quest held at Quinn's Post Hotel in Upper Hutt. Incidentally, this was a pub he says he had been drinking at since he was 13 years old. "A friend of ours entered me and my two sisters, and we thought, 'Oh yeah, there's a $1,000 prize – choice, we'll have a crack,' and we won."

At the time Jon was working at EMI in Lower Hutt, pressing albums. He played rugby league in his spare time. "I loved it and had played since I was six years old, and had been playing in all the rep teams. I wasn't even considering music as a career. It had never even entered my head. But I just happened to get a call from a guy who had heard me sing somewhere, and he said, 'I'm working in a studio and we need a singer for these demo songs. Would you mind coming in and singing them?'

Being a shy polite Maori boy I said, 'Sure, okay.' So I went in and sang them, and he sent them off to CBS and they immediately wanted to sign me. I said I wasn't interested, and they said 'Do you mind if we put one of the songs out?' 'Yeah, I don't care. Go for your life,' I said.

"The song was *Jezebel*, and it ended up being the longest-running number one in New Zealand's history at that time, and I wasn't even signed! I did a couple of other things like *Ready To Roll* and then I had to give up rugby league because every time I ran out on the field there would be this 'Whoa, Jon Stevens – let's bash him eh!' Oh shit, I had to keep fighting while I was playing! So in the end I had to make a choice, thinking this music lark's not too bad."

When Jon left home and came to Australia in early 1981, suddenly everything at home starting changing. "Maori had a currency, there was a pride which I've watched from here in Australia, and I've become the observer of my own people. I go back home all the time and I can see the

Jon Stevens in the '80s

pride, and I see Maori who are educated and are starting to do their thing. When I was a kid I went on the land marches, I was there, I was walking with my family down the highway – I remember all that stuff. And I've got my moko right here on my chest, over my heart. I've had that for 20 years. I have two tattoos, one on my heart and one on my right thumb – UH for Upper Hutt. I did that when I was 12 years old. All my friends had homemade tattoos all over them, and we did the old UH, and I left it there so I would never forget where I came from because I

Jon showing his moko on his chest.

had plans to get out even at that age.

"Wellington has really become quite cosmopolitan, hasn't it? It's caught up, it's grown up. I love the place and I'd love to go back and live there but I'd be bored, probably. I thrive on just doing stuff, and in New Zealand I'd get bored pretty quickly. But I'll retire there, I will always go home. For the record, if I die anywhere in the world, somebody get me and take me back to New Zealand, will ya? Stick my body in New Zealand soil."

Jon's career took off in Australia. He found fame as the front-man of the band Noiseworks and starred in the stage performance of *Jesus Christ Superstar*. He has toured the world as lead singer of INXS and now has a flourishing solo career. All this upheaval has never bothered his children. "Both my kids were born in Australia. They've been home many times. They've been to a couple of tangis, they have experienced the cultural side of things, the spiritual aspect of things, the whole coming together – they understand that. They are modern-day children. They're teenagers now and do all the things that I could never have even dreamed about. My kids are well-travelled. We lived in America for a few years and they're pretty well-rounded. They make no complaints about having to get on a plane.

"I think New Zealanders have a great reputation for being such good travellers. I remember going to America for the first time in 1981 from New Zealand. I was just a kid, really. People would say, 'Where you from?' I would say, 'New Zealand,' and they would say, 'Where's that?' But they don't any more. They know who New Zealanders are now, which is pretty cool."

Jon loves the Australian lifestyle. He lives on one of Sydney's eastern suburb's beaches, and he feels he's picked the best place for his family. Even with an occasional Aussie twang slipping into his language, he dismisses any Australian attempt at ownership with a quick shrug of the shoulders.

"When Australians claim New Zealanders as their own, they just do that to prop themselves up. When I first came here MiSex were really huge, and Dragon, Split Enz, and Sharon O'Neil – there were so many Kiwi musicians they'd claimed. At that time there was quite a lot of animosity, with talk of Kiwi bludgers going on the dole and that kind of stuff, which was shithouse really. I always had to defend myself as a Kiwi and I'd get into so many arguments. That went on until about 1993, and then it changed. Now, in 2007, Aussies have a healthier respect for Kiwis. We've come here and are successful, and they love that. I think the ANZAC thing is true, the Aussies and Kiwis together.

"It's good to hear Maori being spoken when I go home now. These days kids are being brought up to respect the culture, and they have the opportunity to know the language. I wish I'd had that. I wish I'd been able to be more involved. It's fantastic when I see my great-nieces and nephews all speaking the language. I feel humbled."

SHONA  MARTYN

Sitting in her Sydney office of publishers HarperCollins, Shona Martyn is in her ninth year as publishing director, with the Australasian publishing world at her feet. The fact that she is dressed in Trelise Cooper for an interview about New Zealand identity does not go unnoticed.

She freely admits her attachment to the Australian lifestyle – the weather being one of the biggest attractions – but in reality her heart is closer to home. "I do feel very proud of coming from New Zealand – it is a core part of me. I define myself as a person from New Zealand who lives in Sydney. I don't really feel you have to live in a country to feel attached to it."

Shona's schoolteacher father Bruce instilled in her a love of books from an early age. At the end of every week he would present his daughter with a new book in which she happily immersed herself. They were mostly non-fiction books such as *My Home Is in Russia/India/Fiji* and so on, and the popular Ladybird versions of *British Birds and Nests*, and *Costumes Through the Ages* (a particular favourite).

"I also read a lot of fiction, but much of that would have been from the library until I got older and started reading from Dad's vast book collection." Her father would often switch to reading aloud if she came into the room when he was reading and this could have been anything from George Eliot to Iris Murdoch to Conan Doyle. "I often said one of the reasons I was destined for books was the encouragement my father gave me to read," she says.

During Shona's childhood, she spent a lot of time inside reading as she was a sickly asthmatic child, often away from school with bronchitis. "In standard one I was off sick for six weeks with pneumonia, and expected to die. Hilariously, a family friend chose to give me a set of the complete *Pollyanna* books about the saccharine American child who always looked on the bright side. I also missed learning long division but that doesn't seem to have hampered me in terms of doing mega book publishing deals!"

Every two years the Martyn family made a major summer holiday trek to Oamaru – by train and ferry and train – to visit Bruce's family. "Dad was a contemporary of Janet Frame's at school and was very much a proud Oamaruvian – although the only member of his family to leave for university. He was dux of Waitaki Boys' High School in the famous Frank Milner era. Dad's copy of *Owls Do Cry* was annotated with the real names of the characters and places – including the Martyn family bike shop – and he was at the Oamaru swimming baths on the day Janet's sister drowned. Years later he wrote a short story about it and sent it to Janet. Our South Island holidays featured boating on the Kakanui

Shona with her parents, Bruce and Jean Martyn

Not long after starting school

River where the family had a crib, and visits to the cake shop with Great-Aunt Rose, a legendary infant teacher. I found out in recent times that she taught Keri Hulme's mother. Indeed Keri has been known to buy fishing tackle at the family shop, now run by my cousins."

While Bruce Martyn was working as a teacher at St Kentigern's College he was secretly saving to take his family to England for two years. "This was because my father was very much a Europhile. He'd taught French and German and had lived in London and also taught in Switzerland at a posh private school for boys. When he returned he met my mother, Jean, a secretary, who was saving to go with her girlfriends on a trip of a lifetime. They were set up on a blind date to the movies and my mother fell in love and married Dad. So she never did get her trip. Because he loved Europe so much, he knew what she had missed out on. I remember she was furious when she found out he had put a deposit down for us to sail on the *Oriana* because by now she had two children, my brother Peter and me, and was settled in Mt Wellington, Auckland. She didn't feel any need to travel. In fact it is the only time I recall my parents arguing when I was a child. But she did agree to go – and so we did get our trip to England when I was nine and a half, and we returned when I was 11 and about start Form 2 at Remuera Intermediate. We loved being in England – especially Mum. I don't think we would have returned if Dad hadn't been bound to the restrictions of government superannuation."

Shona was an early reader at school. "I had been at school for only six months when I'd read all the books in the infant department at Stanhope Road Primary School. I was the only girl still in Primary who was allowed to use the Standards' library. Later I went to Epsom Grammar. It was a good school but I don't think it brought out my full potential. It may be hard to believe now but I was a rather shy teenager. I had quite low self-esteem until I got rid of my glasses in the 7th Form. I think I could have benefited if I'd had a little bit more individual attention although I did enjoy the competition of being pitted against other smart girls.

"For a long time I assumed when I left school I would become a teacher since teachers ran in the family. However, my mother was by then working in an administrative role on a small newspaper and she suggested that journalism might be the sort of thing I'd enjoy. It sounded fantastic to me as it was fast-paced and every day was different. I set my mind on applying for the ATI journalism course and began submitting stories to my local newspaper. By the time I went to the interview I had a scrapbook full and told them that if they turned me down then I would keep re-applying until I got in. Persistence is an advantage in journalism."

Shona says she has always been ambitious, and although she had no definite plan she supposed she'd eventually work overseas. "I started as a cadet at the *Auckland Star* in its heyday, the time of the Arthur Allan Thomas and Mr Asia cases. I was the cadet reporter sitting behind these guys who would be making arrangements to interview all manner of dubious people for the story. There was rumoured to be a contract out on (deputy editor) Pat Booth's life. It was a fantastic time in terms of inspiration. It was also a very idealistic time. There was a sense that journalism could make a difference. There was Watergate and *All the President's Men*. There was *Lou Grant* on television. After three years at the *Star*, I worked another two years at the *New Zealand Herald* – covering education, the health round and politics – when I won the Qantas Journalist of the Year Award for a portfolio of stories. I was only 23 and the prize was a return trip to United Kingdom. I cashed it in and made it two one-way tickets and then Steve Crane, my boyfriend of the time, and I got married ("to make us respectable") and left the country. I didn't imagine I'd return to live in New Zealand. It was 1981 and there was no *Metro* or *North and South* then so if I'd stayed I'd really only have continued with newspaper work and, at 23, I needed a bigger horizon."

The couple spent a year at Montserrat in the Caribbean, where her Wellington-born husband had miraculously got a job at Beatles producer George Martin's famous Air recording studio. Shona read books and hung out with rock stars such as Elton John and his entourage, and then they had a stint in London where she worked as features editor of a local newspaper. The couple moved to Sydney in 1983. A job as a feature writer at *Vogue* fitted in with her love of clothes and gave her colour magazine experience. She then moved to senior editorial roles at *Good Weekend*, the prestigious colour supplement of the *Sydney Morning Herald* and *The Age* before being offered the opportunity to create a new serious glossy for Australian Consolidated Press. *HQ* magazine, which Shona edited for seven years, won numerous awards and gained both critical acclaim and a cult following. In 1996 came the offer of the role of publisher for Transworld Publishers (now part of Random House). "I decided I didn't have anything to lose – I could always have gone back to journalism if it didn't work out." Three years later she was headhunted by HarperCollins for a new role of publishing director – which encompasses overseeing all local publications as well as a large department of specialist publishers, designers, contract administrators, editors, production people and so on.

Shona, second from right, with work colleagues on Sydney harbour

"I am part of international publishing in this role and a very competitive world it is too," says Shona, citing a recent work trip that encompassed New York, Frankfurt for its Book Fair, Paris and London.

About seven years ago, Shona volunteered to expand her role to get involved in HarperCollins' New Zealand operation. "I felt I had the opportunity to give something back to New Zealand." Conveniently this allows her to travel to Auckland every six weeks for book acquisition meetings – with the benefit of being able to visit family and friends. "As I am involved in buying books for New Zealand publication, it is essential I keep up with what is going on there." Christopher Read, son of TV's *Night Sky* presenter, Peter Read, is her current partner. "We've been together since 1989, and it wasn't really until we had our daughter Evangeline in 1995 that we started going home a lot more for holidays. He's a music publisher and works with a number of New Zealand bands so we both have a strong work connection with New Zealand. I wouldn't have gone out with a man who wasn't from New Zealand. I do have standards!" And she laughs.

"Evangeline's most memorable early holiday experiences have been New Zealand beach holidays, particularly at Whangaparoua on the Coromandel, thanks to generous friends. As a first-generation child, Evangeline identifies strongly with New Zealand. I think she sees herself as special, although there's always a mixed feeling – for instance, who do you support in football games? She certainly sees herself as both an Australian and a New Zealander. I find that in Australia people generally identify me as a New Zealander because of my accent. While it varies – I can be very 'English' on the phone – it can be quite strong at times, especially after a glass of wine or if I am with other New Zealanders. Of course not a week will go by in the Sydney office without jokes about New Zealanders. And vice versa.

"Overseas, at things like the annual Frankfurt Book Fair, people see me as an Australian. They can't tell the difference in the accents. If for some reason I reveal I am from New Zealand, there is often a lot more curiousity because most people have a keen desire to visit the country. And, of course, HarperCollins is the publisher of *Lord of the Rings*!

"One aspect I find interesting in the Australian-New Zealand relationship is that most Australians think that New Zealanders secretly wish they were Australian. What they don't realise is that New Zealanders feel sorry for Australians – the last thing they would want to be is Australian! You see, Australia has a big-country perspective, and they think that if something is from New Zealand it's small and trivial. New Zealand on the other hand has an elitist, best-country-in the-world kind of attitude and they feel sorry for other people who aren't them.

"Australia's indifference towards anything New Zealand extends into the publishing business. In many instances, when a book comes out of New Zealand the Australian booksellers will say, 'Oh! It's from New Zealand. Not for us, thanks.' This is the equivalent of saying it's from a small daggy place, and why would we want to read it? The breakthrough comes with authors like Elizabeth Knox who has had global success or, of course, *Mr Pip* by Lloyd Jones who is picking up international prizes. Mind you, the same happens in New Zealand. New Zealand bookshops say, 'Why would we want to read Australian authors? We have New Zealand authors who are so much better.'

"There are New Zealand books we've de-Kiwified – for want of a better word – for the Australian market. Books that have been a huge success in New Zealand and have used a lot of Maori words – which in New Zealand you could use in a totally normal non-italicised kind of way. But if you put that into an Australian book, people wouldn't know what you were talking about. This of course applies only to non-fiction. A few authors are already trying to get around this by writing for an 'international' market. That is, they don't say where the person lives. In many cases, though, to do this would undermine the impact of the book in, say, the New Zealand market, and this would not be a good idea. In any country, it is best to write for your local audience first, not to compromise for the sake of possible sales elsewhere. After all, if your books are good, revised editions are possible."

If a book became hugely successful, or was highly original or an international award winner – such issues obviously fell away. What would really help would be less prejudice by readers, booksellers and reviewers on both sides of the Tasman, Shona says.

Other aspects of New Zealand cultural endeavours are more flexible.

Nobody thinks, 'Oh, it's a New Zealand film,' and dismisses it. Fashion is another. A lot of her friends, both Australian and New Zealand, say with pride that they wear only New Zealand clothes. "New Zealand designers are seen as being far more innovative than Australian designers." New Zealand food and wine are obviously seen as world-class.

Shona finds it "interesting and encouraging" how New Zealanders are now enunciating Maori words. "When I'm in meetings in Auckland I'm the one who can't pronounce the words correctly. But I listen to my mother and the correct pronuniciation of Maori words now trips off her tongue. New Zealand is a better place for this, but there was a myth in the '60s that everything was perfect. For those of us growing up then, there was very much the sense that the term 'lucky country' for Australia was coined in an ironic way and that it wasn't. New Zealand genuinely saw itself as that, and I remember in primary school being told we were the only country that had no race relations problems! It must have been insulting for the Maori, Pacific Island or Chinese people who were sitting among us who might have thought otherwise.

"New Zealand has been hugely helped by its early adoption of feminism. The number of women in positions of power is testament to that. Primarily it's because of the migrant population make-up in New Zealand compared with Australia where women still have a harder row to hoe in getting into senior positions. My personal theory is that Scottish-Presbyterian matriarchs had a lot to do with it. People like my grandmother of the Temperance Union – those women controlled the purse strings. My father, growing up in Oamaru in the 1920s, had four siblings. Four boys and one daughter, and my father and his brothers always helped with the housework. Even after he married, Dad always did the dishes and he would also peel the vegetables as he got home from work earlier than my mum. I used to live in fear that my friends might see him in an apron.

"Ironically, these days due to the pressure of my work I leave the bulk of the cooking to Christopher even though I can cook well myself. Mind you, he doesn't wear an apron! And he is an excellent cook.

"So I think the Scottish matriarch allowed things to be set up so well that, when the 1970s came along, women who were 10 years older than me were very able to take advantage of opportunities.

"When I fly over to New Zealand – especially in business class – you can usually pick who are the Australians and who are the New Zealanders. If there are executive women, they are likely to be New Zealanders and they tend to wear edgier clothing and have more cutting-edge hairstyles and jewellery. Although I am afraid that too many New Zealand women are overdoing the dangling earrings! The rarer counterparts in Australia are still trying to match the men in corporate wear – suits, non-funky hair and jewellery. Women are less hampered in New Zealand because they are a good 10 years ahead of Australian women in terms of opportunities. I also feel it's incredibly inspiring to have a woman prime minister and of course other women in key leadership positions, and that until Australia has women at these most senior levels, it will be harder for other younger women to follow."

Her own assertiveness, Shona thinks, has helped her in dealing with such people as the sometimes aggressive international literary agents. She works in a very competitive industry, "and you can't exactly be a shrinking violet." A lot of her job is problem-solving, and managing

Shona with author Ben Elton at a sales conference in the Blue Mountains

expectations of authors and making them feel positive about themselves. She also is determined to do everything she can to make their books bestsellers. "I have found books to be more exciting than magazines. I did newspapers in my twenties, magazines in my thirties and now books are the perfect career. It's an industry where you can't predict what is going to happen on any given day."

From a book publisher's point of view, Shona says New Zealand has the strongest book-buying public in the world. "It is a very educated population. I know of overseas colleagues who are amazed at how many copies of books New Zealand's small population can absorb."

She feels one of the things about a country you've grown up in, and left, is that you think of the landscape you've left behind as the best and most beautiful landscape there is. "I can get teary-eyed even flying into Auckland. I'm very attached to New Zealand visually – we have embraced that *Pasifika* style of homewares. I notice that a lot of ex-pat New Zealanders put stuff up in our houses that reminds us of home. There's that aesthetic there that is special, that we connect with on a visceral level.

"But what is irritating about New Zealanders to me is their perverted sense of rights. That there could be opposition to a ban on using a mobile phone while driving because it infringed rights – even though all evidence and experience says it is dangerous. Things like, 'I'll drive at the speed limit in the fast lane and I don't care what anybody behind me thinks.' Yeah, we're terrible drivers, and, as someone who commutes for an hour each way both in Sydney and Auckland, I know that traffic moves more quickly in Australia because people know how to merge lanes and even do so with friendly waves. But at the same time there is a goody-goody streak, with people returning their trolleys at the airport or supermarket which doesn't happen in Australia. These are contradictions which I find amusing. There's also a hilarious degree of pessimism in terms of how many New Zealanders look at things – the glass is always half empty."

For Shona there is something about the land and the scenery that creative people pick up on. She particularly sees it in fashion and the colours that New Zealand designers use. "There's a slight gothic sensibility – although it's not a thing that's unique to New Zealand. You see it in

Belgium, in Portugal and possibly in Canada. Could it be something about living in the shadow of a larger land?

"I still don't think that I will ever return to live, although Evangeline would like to. With the work that Christopher and I do, I don't think that parallel roles exist for us there and we are not looking at phasing back or winding down. Perhaps It would be different if I was a doctor – patients would be as challenging in both countries. Work is one of the most significant drives in my life. But then there's the weather ..."

She doesn't get very homesick these days because of her regular trips home. But when she first left New Zealand for London there was one time when it almost became too much. "I got very upset when I saw the demonstrations over the Springbok Tour on the TV news. It was so awfully wrong. Now we just feel homesick for the culture and the music. But things like that can be portable – we play *Fat Freddy's Drop* and *Wai* at home for example.

"In January 2006 we went to a combined 50th birthday party at Awaroa Lodge in the Abel Tasman National Park. There were guests from around the world. It was a whole lodge full of 50-year-old ex-pat New Zealanders. I found an incredible degree of similarity about us. We had travelled for various reasons and some, although not all, had not come back to live which I found very interesting. It may be different with people a decade younger who had more opportunities to embrace New Zealand in their 20s.

"I find ex-pat New Zealanders all have this fondness for New Zealand, stronger say, than what you see in English people who migrate to Australia. I find I look out for New Zealanders who come my way. I have been inclined – more in the past when I was editing magazines – to let somebody come in and pitch their ideas if they were from New Zealand! Call it positive discrimination, or a free kick."

PETER GORDON

PETER GORDON IS ONE OF NEW ZEALAND'S MOST HIGHLY ACCLAIMED CHEFS overseas. Almost all his memories are associated with food, naturally enough. His London restaurant The Providores, boasts fusion dining with many dishes containing New Zealand grown ingredients, and he champions Kiwi produce whenever he has the opportunity. He also consults to, and oversees, two Auckland restaurants – one called dine by Peter Gordon, and the other, the Spanish tapas bar, Bellota, and he also has an interest in an Otago vineyard.

He returns to New Zealand four times a year and while freely admitting to New Zealand being the 'most beautiful country in the world,' he worries about the 'gothic' undercurrent. "I'll go home for three weeks and it always seems there are ten people murdered, by someone on P or some child beaten to death. It's like 'Oh my God!'"

Peter left New Zealand in 1981 for Australia where he stayed five years, working as a chef in Melbourne. After traveling through Asia he returned to Wellington to set up the kitchen at The Sugar Club restaurant for its two owners. Next he headed to London in 1989 where finally in 1995 and 1998 he set up two more Sugar Club kitchens. He left the Sugar Club in 1999 and opened The Providores with his partner and two friends in 2001. With five self-authored recipe books in print, his role as consultant chef to two award-winning restaurants in Istanbul, and in constant demand for appearances on television food shows, both in the UK and in New Zealand, he has shown no limits to his success.

"Mum and dad divorced when I was four, Rose my step-mum, and Dad are the most wonderful people – supportive and non-judgemental. They have remained living in Wanganui where I was brought up. Mum and my first stepfather lived up in Auckland – although I never really got on with him. Mum remarried for the third time ten years ago, and I've now got a fantastic stepfather so I think I'm very lucky. My mum is a fantastic woman and I feel as if I've got four of the best parents."

Peter grew up in Castlecliff, a beachside suburb of Wanganui, his father, Bruce Gordon, an engineer, had his own business. "A lot of his friends worked at the Imlay Freezing Works and I would come home sometimes and there would be a carcass hanging up in the garage. It was a ridiculously huge four car garage with a 15 foot ceiling and there would often be an oxen and a couple of sheep hanging from the rafters. Dad and his freezing work mates would have already removed the guts at the freezing works. They would chop the carcass up into joints, and we would render the fat down and make soap for dad's workshop. I used to watch but I was never allowed to take part – the chemicals and the axes were a bit too much, I think. One year my half brother Craig threw a whole lot of the soap in the swimming pool overnight and when we got up in the morning the backyard was covered in soap suds.

"We'd fry all our fish and chips in the beef fat – they were yummy – but the chips never got crispy. Up in Auckland my mum would cook her fish and chips in oil and I used to think it was so glamorous. They were more shoe string and crispy and I loved that. That's when I thought, 'Oh yeah, there is a difference!' This was something I discovered when I was about eight or nine."

Peter's first memory of cooking is making an apple pie with his mother when he was just four. "I know that sounds a very American memory but it's where it all began, I think. When Mum moved to Auckland, then later New Plymouth she'd make sure the butcher aged her meat – especially a rolled boned leg of lamb or the beef rib eye. Mum's approach to food made me realise that it wasn't just a commodity." He began cutting recipes out of *Woman's Weekly*. "I was making up a scrap-book. Instead of it being All Blacks and tennis players, it was soufflé omelettes and béchamel sauce – all very French, I remember. I don't know where that scrap-book has gone but it would be wonderful to find it again!"

"Meal times were quite different in both my families. In Wanganui with Dad and Rose it was a very practical time – we'd all been working or at school and Rose would be expected to churn out meal after meal for anywhere between seven and nine people. I don't know how she did it, to be honest. Once Dad won custody of the kids, the only time I spent at Mum's house was during the holidays, so it seemed more relaxed. Mum was a really good cook, producing lovely light tasty food. Years later she opened and managed cafes and food venues. She still makes the most amazing slices, cakes and the like. Her husband Clyde is a great barbecue man and he loves fishing – he and Dad have a lot in common actually. Rose makes the best corned beef and her bacon and egg pies are legendary, and Dad is famous for his soufflé omelettes. No wonder with these people as my parents, along with my three food-obsessed sisters, food was in my genes."

When Peter was seven, he was helping his father to deep-fry fish and chips with oysters. While the rest of the family were distracted he decided to check out the progress of the meal. "I got up on a little stool, trying to balance myself as it had the rubber off one of the legs, but it wobbled and I started to fall," he says. Unhappily he grabbed hold of the deep fryer to keep steady, and in doing so poured boiling fat over his body. "Dad heard the noise and ran into the kitchen, slipped on the oil and slid across the floor, burning his knees. Everyone else came running out into the kitchen and my sister Vicki started screaming. Rose, who was still only our housekeeper at the time, was bathing her two kids. I remember they were left in the bathtub while all the drama was going on – luckily they didn't drown. Rose got on to the doctor and asked what they should do – should they throw me in the swimming pool? He said no and to call an ambulance right away. We waited for ages and it hadn't come so we got into the car and drove there with me wrapped in a blanket. As we drove into the Wanganui Base Hospital the car was almost side-swiped by the ambulance as it was roaring out to come and get me. I was quickly taken into A&E, and smothered with cream. While this was happening I had an out-of-body experience. Even now I can still picture myself in that hospital room – it was as if I was up in the corner of the ceiling looking down at

Peter, 13, as a schoolboy in Wanganui

myself under a metal cage to keep the fabric off my burns, with green sheets on top. I was put on painkillers, and I remember people coming in to visit while I was in a private room because of risk of infection. My sister Tracey came in and burst into tears. None of the memories are bad. I guess it was because no one around me was hysterical. I have a feeling my body just went into shock – slowed right down and I kept quite calm."

After he was released from hospital, Peter was able to go back to school provided he wore a sunhat while outside, and he had to wear a tee-shirt while swimming. "Can you imagine a seven-year-old Kiwi kid wearing a straw wide-brimmed hat among other kids who wouldn't even think of wearing sunhats? That's when I got picked on." I was a tiny little kid but made up for it by being a pretty good fighter. I was one of those fighters who when I was picked on, although I had no brawn, could jump on someone, and I wouldn't let go. After a few weeks they stopped."

"Even now I'll be on the tube in London and there will be some kid gawking at me. Their parents tell them not to stare and I'll usually go over and talk to the kids. The parents look worried, understandably, or embarrassed, but usually grateful at the end of it. The scar is all down the right side of my neck – luckily it missed my ears, and my eyes weren't damaged. I remember being taken aside on my first day of intermediate school and being told by the headmaster that because of my – I remember the word 'deformity' – I would be the only boy in school who was allowed to grow my hair long. I'm gay nowadays and when I look back I wonder what must my parents have been thinking? 'He's saving soufflé recipes and he's growing his hair long – how can he not turn out queer?'" he says with a laugh.

He says he doesn't think he knew he was gay; he didn't know any gay people and therefore didn't know what gay was. "I was kind of aware, though, while all the boys would be talking about all the girls I was thinking 'Oh I don't get it!' I've since found out that a few people I went to school and university with are gay. Others have been in touch with me over the years and as soon as I mention I'm gay I never hear from most of them again. Maybe I grew up with a whole lot of homophobes! The only gay New Zealanders I was aware of were Hudson and Halls on TV and a guy who was transferred to my school – Wanganui High School – from Boys' College I think it was. Our headmaster called a meeting for all the male students and told us we weren't to pick on this new guy. Which of course made everyone in the assembly room want to know more. I also remember, aged about 12, seeing an episode of *Whicker's World* where Alan Whicker spent time with the 'homosexual community' somewhere in the USA and they all looked quite normal to me. It wasn't until I went to Australia and started cooking and met 'out and proud' gay people that I thought 'Oh, what's all this?'

"When I look back, had it been possible to discuss sexuality as a child, it would have been quite different. As it was, when I grew up as a teenager in Wanganui, all the other boys talked about snogging the girls because that's what we did at school dances. I did my fair share of it, but never really enjoyed it. It wasn't a big deal for me because, again, my parents didn't really give a shit about anything – they just liked good people." It's different for kids growing up now, or so he hopes, because of better attitudes in schools.

He had two different childhoods. His mother lived up on Auckland's North Shore and they drove around in Jags and lived in big houses. "They were always two-storey and had lots of trees around them and they all drank wine – in those days it was Mozelle. Back in Wanganui we drove around in a very daggy, but cool, Chevy Impala. It was a huge thing. We went on camping holidays and Dad and Rose drank beer out of flagons.

I'm so glad I lived in Wanganui. It was just great. All through summer Dad and his mates would go out fishing and would put the nets out on summer evenings. We'd go down to the beach and help them bring the boat back before school at 6.30 or 7.00 in the morning, helping them fillet the fish and bring it home. Then my stepmum would cook some breakfast. We would pick some passion-fruit off the vine and cycle off to school. I kind of thought it was all quite normal. Living out at Castlecliff you felt like it was a small village on its own. We seemed to live through egalitarian times in the '60s and '70s, we had plenty of food and even though Dad and my stepmum were never broke they weren't well off. "

Peter is part-Maori and when he was 21 he went to a family reunion at Papawai marae near Greytown, for Ngati Kahungunu. "I was so looking forward to it, but the only people who looked vaguely Maori were the people our family had married." The first white person on his father's side was John Stenton Workman from Scotland who married a Maori called Ellen Rewhaunga (Kokoriti) in 1853. This means Peter is 1/32 Maori. "My great-grandmother – I can still remember her – she and my grandmother were part of the first wave of Maori-Pakeha unions. I love the fact that I have Maori blood in me. I wish I had more." Peter's paternal grandmother was Molly Gordon who lived on the hills of Strathmore in Wellington. Molly set up the charity called After Care. "My dad had been one of three kids, and the middle child, my Auntie Mary, had had a terrible reaction to whooping cough vaccine and became mentally impaired when she was about seven, so Gran created this charity to help get people back into the community. When the Queen was in New Zealand one year she gave her a QSM medal. Gran was this wonderful woman who thought that the world is a community. She felt that everybody has a responsibility and we should do what we can. It is the philosophy that I grew up with, and to this day it's what I live by.

"When I go back to New Zealand I feel so at home, and going back to Wanganui is always a pleasure. I think it is the most beautiful country in the world. There's something about it, the earth there seems to emanate a vibration that just seems to hum. It's the only time I feel the earth is alive."

Peter and his partner Michael McGrath have invested in a winery in

Waitaki, North Otago, called Waitaki Braids, and along with dine and Bellota in Auckland there is still a very strong pull back to New Zealand. This extends to his London menu.

"I'm always on the lookout for Kiwi ingredients, such as kawakawa, horopito, korengo, kumara and Seresin olive oil. Our wine list is always 85 percent Kiwi, and it's the largest premium New Zealand-led wine list in Europe, that I'm aware of. That's a deliberate thing for us, we are always very aware of Kiwi products – we happily want to showcase New Zealand.

"It's 'quite straight forward, really. We'll get people who come in and say, 'Oh my God, you're Kiwis – we didn't have any idea,' and we get other people who come in and say, 'We heard you were a Kiwi restaurant.' We have many dishes that aren't Kiwi, but probably if you're at a table of four at least two of the ingredients or influences will be Kiwi. There could be hokey-pokey ice-cream or my grandmother's caramel slice or her shortbread on your biscuit plate. Some people probably wouldn't

Photo: Brent Derby

Peter in the kitchen

102

pick up on it, but there are some who will get it straight away.

"Often, if we've had a review, New Zealand usually gets mentioned somewhere, or if they are writing about me they will say 'New Zealander Peter Gordon,' – I love it. Recently I did some filming on a show here called *Great Food Live*, which I do every now and again, and on one show I had 42 Below Vodka, manuka and rata honey, kumara and freeze-dried herbs from FRESH AS in Auckland."

Many of the restaurant's dishes are created by the chef team. Until recently, of the 11 chefs, 10 were Kiwis and one was an Aussie, and now there are a Thai, Mauritian, an Englishman and eight Kiwis. "Thank God we got rid of some of the Kiwis!" he says with a laugh. "All they ever played on the stereo was Crowded House and Salmonella Dub, and all the jokes were the same. Bro Town was our inspiration for kitchen speak – personally I align myself with Geoff the Maori. The way our kitchen works is we encourage everyone to come up with ideas and we'll learn something from them and they learn from us. So I suppose the kitchen ethos is very Kiwi, it's very egalitarian. Say if we have 50 items on the menus, 20 to 25 of them are mine or inspired by me, and the remainder are from the other chefs, mainly our head chef Miles Kirby and our sous chef Cristian Hossack – both Kiwis. We probably have about 22 different wine suppliers, managed by our third partner, Jeremy Leeming, which we need to have in order to get the variety of New Zealand wines we want. Unlike a supplier of French wines who will list many Burgundy reds, say, most UK suppliers will just represent one Otago Pinot Noir producer.

"A really hot topic at present is food miles. The English press query why the Brits should buy New Zealand lamb when they produce lamb themselves? If England is worried about food miles, then they are going to have to stop importing coffee and tea, vanilla, ginger, mangos and so on. Plus they should stop exporting food if they're going to be serious about it. Britain can produce only around 65-75 percent of the food it needs, and during November through to Easter they don't produce lamb, which is when chilled New Zealand lamb comes in. They need to re-think their attitude towards us because if they are going to slag off the produce from New Zealand they better be prepared to go hungry because it's likely they are still going to have to use our food. Practically all the electricity in New Zealand required to produce food has zero or negligible carbon emissions as most of the electricity comes from hydro schemes. However, in the UK almost all of the energy is carbon-based – and they kind of forget things such as a container ship coming from New Zealand burns less carbon per ton of food than a lorry from Wales or Scotland."

Peter is interested in the subject of the English class system compared with the lack thereof in New Zealand. "What I notice about the Kiwis I mix with here in London is that we are aware of the bigger picture of society. We intrinsically have a community feel about us – we are a community rather than being individuals. Nearly everyone I know has this thing of not knowing where to place themselves, knowing that New Zealand is the most beautiful place on earth but not necessarily wanting to go back to live permanently because of the quietness and isolation."

He observes that there are far too many murders in New Zealand, and that there appears to be a 'gothic' undercurrent. "All the movies that get made there are quite gothic, such as *In My Father's Den*, *The Piano* and *Heavenly Creatures*. I can remember way back in the '60s and '70s when Mona Blades went missing, and the Crewe murders happened. In the 'old days' something like this might have happened maybe every two years or so. Murders are all too frequent now, especially with child victims, and it's a worry.

"Every other Kiwi I know here talks – ad nauseam – about the fact they want to live the summers there and the summers here. To me it was always a definite. I would go back to New Zealand to retire. Then I began to ask myself, just because you are old, do you want to live in retirement on a beach in the sun and get skin cancer? Maybe when I'm older I'll have some free time to hang out in New Zealand, but meanwhile I love the stimulation that living in a city like London offers."

When Peter returns home on his frequent visits he generally finds people are interested when he talks about his London life. However there are others who will turn away. "I'm not bragging about my life! Maybe it's an isolation thing. Some New Zealanders seem to think that because you've left you're never going to come back and so you must have to give up your identity, but that's stupid – if anything, you are more aware of your identity when you leave. When I was first cooking in London,

Photo: Sue Campbell

Peter Gordon

people would come and visit and they were proud of me being a Kiwi and waving the flag. But when I'm back in New Zealand and opening a restaurant in Auckland, some of them don't even bother to look me up any more. It's as though they think *I* might think they're a loser and that they haven't gone and done something with their life overseas – but that's not what I think. Some of our closest friends live in New Zealand and we go back and hang out and have a really nice time, but there are some people who ... oh, I don't know, I wish I could figure it out.

"In my career I've worked very hard and absolutely nothing has ever been handed to me on a plate. My parents never supported me financially, they didn't need to once I'd left home, but they were always there emotionally and they instilled in me some very good core values, as my gran had done to my father. After 18 years of living in London I've built a niche for myself, and being a gay Kiwi with a burnt face doing fusion food which no one else really does, it's hardly like I've taken an easy path."

TRELISE COOPER

TRELISE COOPER SPENDS A GOOD PART OF EVERY YEAR OVERSEAS, BUT BE IT BUSINESS or pleasure she is always happy to be back home in New Zealand. Her success is well known but there are some pitfalls – such as being cut down to size for being just that bit too successful. "I come across the tall poppy syndrome all the time in New Zealand. I could name so many examples where I've been attacked for doing well. You find you're spending a lot of time defending yourself."

But there are many other things she loves about the place. "I think it is great that we are not too close to US policy, as Australia is. I like it that we have a nuclear-free policy and we are free of the obligation to the US. We've taken a wider view, which can only be good. "

Growing up in Auckland, Trelise says she had an "okay education". She didn't find school at all inspiring. "I didn't know it at the time but I was above average intelligence, although the schools I went to didn't recognise it. My dad always said I needed a skill behind me like short-hand typing – office work was considered a good choice for girls in those days. In the fifth form at Henderson High School I was put in the academic class – it was discovered I could do more than the kids doing the commercial subjects such as book-keeping. I was disappointed when I was put in with the 'brainies' because I felt I had nothing in common with them. I got School Certificate and that's all I needed to leave school. When I look at the education my son Jasper – who's now at university in Melbourne – has had, I can see it was a completely different experience for him. He's had a lot of choices.

"When I left school I didn't know much about anything. I sometimes look back on those days in wonderment at how I got to be where I am today. I didn't even know what a receptionist was when I got a job as one. I couldn't believe how that meant I got paid to go to work and answer a phone. I loved that. There were job opportunities that involved typing but all I wanted to do was look nice and answer the phones.

"I got a job in a shoe factory where I could answer the phone and be the house model – it was my absolute dream job. The girl I grew up with next door went nursing in Texas. She's still there, but that didn't appeal to me at all. I had no inclination to leave New Zealand and go anywhere."

She became engaged just after her 16th birthday, and married just after her 17th. "It was what I wanted to do. I wanted to make babies when I was young, but I didn't get pregnant. The marriage lasted five years and then I met my present husband, Jack, and we've now been together for 27 years. I had Jasper when I was 31 – the term they used was 'elderly mother'. The rest of my family had babies at 18. I really thought I'd do what my parents had done, and be young, youthful with my children."

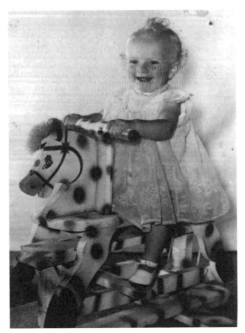

Trelise as a youngster

"Mum and Dad got married as teenagers, and Dad had a drainage contracting business. His first job out of school was with an ad agency, and he was very successful. But he soon had a young family to support and went into something more lucrative. He had a lot more creative potential that didn't get explored. Creativity wasn't even spoken about in my peer group when I was growing up. I know I struggled for a long time to find a female role model.

"It never crossed my mind I'd have to go overseas to be creative. I've always felt I was very much a Kiwi girl and I find it easy to work here. I travel a great deal and I love coming home to New Zealand. I love the fact I don't have overseas experience – although I've had a lot of inspiration from overseas. From 1980 until now I've probably travelled overseas a minimum of four times a year. For the first time I've felt in the past six months I could go and live overseas. We spend a lot of time in France and I do love it there."

When Trelise started out she was unaware of special designer pattern-making courses that she could have taken advantage of. "I'm happy not to have had that formal training because it meant I had no constraints about what I could do. I was breaking down those rules and people were saying, 'You can't do that' and I'm saying, 'Well, why not? Could we at least try?' That freedom to question was important to me.

"I suffered self-doubt for many years. It probably wasn't until six years ago that I acknowledged that something must be working. I think that's a hangover from not having had recognised training. I'm very well trained now, but in an unconventional way. I call it an intuitive knowing. It's looking at a design and knowing if it's going to sell."

Trelise observes that when style influences come in from overseas they are quickly absorbed and then everyone moves on to the next trend. "I find that, with fashion, if orange is in, it's in – but it won't be in next year. There's just over four million people here in New Zealand, and they are going to buy it for this season. If you come out with the same colour again next season it probably won't sell. It's different in Australia. I find if you do one colour there this season, you can use that same colour again the next season. I remember when eftpos came in. We were soon using it, but it took about three more years for Australia to adopt it. I was surprised at how ahead the New Zealand banking system was. I think we are true pioneers. Our background contains the pioneering spirit and that comes through in the way we approach business."

The first thing she notices when she arrives back in New Zealand is the clear air. "Everything is so green and clean. It's probably why I've never done an OE. I think I'd really miss living in New Zealand if I settled somewhere else. I like the fact that you can action an idea really quickly here. I think that's the difference with doing business in New Zealand as opposed to Australia or the US. They think about a project or campaign for a long time before anything is done. My Australian agent said to me one day, 'You know, I think we need a diffusion line with a little more lifestyle.' As he was telling me over the phone I was writing it down and by the time he came over six weeks later I presented him with the new range and he was speechless that I had acted so quickly on his suggestion. "Lately I've been wanting to put a parade on in New York, and I'm clear I can make it happen, but I've had to pull out because I hadn't allowed enough time for the way New York works. I was told by the American PR guy, 'This is not New Zealand. You can't just decide to do something and expect to bring it about in a short time.' Here we have much more freedom to interact with people and get things done quickly. We don't have all the bureaucracy."

New Zealanders have a special creativity because of living at the edge of the world, she thinks "There is a creative quirkiness. Often we can't just go down the road to buy something to put on a garment because it won't be available – we have to recreate it ourselves. The other part to that is because we are a small population we haven't had Gap, Banana Republic or Gucci on our doorstep as every other country in the world has, and I think this forms a platform for original thought. I've always said New Zealand is a fantastic training ground for going global. What happens in fashion elsewhere is that style ends up looking the same, and I believe that individuality is the success of New Zealand fashion."

In US stores, Trelise Cooper designs get offered together with those from all over the world. She says the fact that she's from New Zealand is "cute and a little mysterious, but does it sell? I was talking to Kevin Roberts –World CEO of Saatchi and Saatchi – recently, and he said it's great to be a New Zealander in America at the moment, and it is. But while that mystery may have got me in the door, that's just part of it. I know that if they don't like what you are showing this season, you don't go back in. It's as clear cut as that.

"They always say, 'Oh, I'd love to come down there.' In the past five or so years I think they've finally discovered we're not part of Australia. New Zealand is seen as profoundly different from any place else and that has a lot of pull with the people whom I deal with. I'm acutely aware I have to keep that point of difference that got me in the door."

She is very proud of her New Zealand heritage, and the country is definitely in her heart when she travels. "When I'm away so much I miss the New Zealand summers and I often feel very homesick. I don't like to leave behind the lifestyle that we have. Other times I feel homesick are when a TV set has been on somewhere and I've caught the haka at

Trelise at Australian Fashion Week

the beginning of a rugby match. I remember once I was on a train in London and a Maori kapa haka group got on and we all said hello. I felt quite nostalgic. We should acknowledge our heritage and we should be considered as one people. We are all New Zealanders. I think that the dividing of the country over race issues is dangerous. I don't like a 'them and us' situation.

"New Zealanders are friendly and open and helpful in positive ways. I strongly believe we need Kiwis to succeed as it breeds more success. If there's a negative side to us it would be the tall poppy chopping. I have definitely experienced that on a daily basis. I always describe New Zealand as a village and you get that with village life. But I think it's a real shame. There's quite a lot of envy. It comes from a society which is egalitarian, and if anybody pops up above it then they need to be cut down to their rightful level – I'd be lying if I said it doesn't hurt. I was sitting with my husband in the sun one morning outside our beach house and some people were walking by. I could hear them saying, 'Oh that's Trelise Cooper's house. That's a ridiculous house to have at the beach.' It's our house, it's not a bach, and I feel very lucky that I can live in a house like this.

"Recently a guy who is an Auckland marketing lecturer wrote in a marketing magazine that in order to be invited to my children's store you had to be rich. He was denigrating all these people who could afford to buy my clothes. How ridiculous! I'm not going to invite the unemployed who can't afford to shop there. The article made absolutely no sense and it was scary that it was written by someone who should have known better. This lecturer doesn't live the sort of life he thinks I live – he wanted to cut me down. I see my brand as inclusive. I don't care who my customer is. I treat them all equally. But as a marketing move, yes, I did invite people who had shopped in my store and others who looked as if they would like to shop there. I pitched my brand at those people – that's good marketing. To me his attitude came from resentment of my success. I've had a lot of people say to me, 'Oh you're really nice', and I say, 'Well, yes.' What were they thinking before they met me?"

There are probably many reasons why envy is an unfortunate Kiwi trait, Trelise says. " Talkback in New Zealand has a lot to answer for.

That for me is the beginnings of it – it's all those people without a vested interest in the country who get on it. I hate talkback radio being played at work. It really bothers me. It's this petty small-thinking I detest. But, you know, New Zealand is generally made up of big thinkers. Those who haven't succeeded haven't thought about it enough. I really believe that what you think about is what you create, and it's all that getting on talkback and moaning – it's self-perpetuating. But other than that, I'm a happy New Zealander."

TODD HUNTER

TODD HUNTER ALONG WITH HIS BROTHER MARC GREW UP IN TAUMARANUI, and became the mainstays of the rock band Dragon. Embroiled in the 1970s in drugs and wild times, the band weathered the '80s and '90s but finally imploded when Marc died in 1998. As Todd has made his home in Sydney since 1975, he has immersed himself in Australian life.

"I have very mixed feelings about New Zealand. Every time I returned in the '70s and '80s I would get really fuzzy, as if a dense fog had descended over my head and I couldn't think clearly," he says. "Maybe it's something to do with all the unprocessed issues of my childhood." It's taken five years of therapy, and a recent tour of New Zealand, with the newly re-formed Dragon, to exorcise those demons and to understand and enjoy the country he left behind.

Todd describes growing up in Taumaranui as wild and weird. "Incomprehensible things would happen against the backdrop of idyllic countryside. In the '50s and '60s New Zealand was still very much a British colony, and the Second World War was still on everyone's mind. *Z Cars* and *Coronation Street* were on TV and when the Queen visited we were all herded down to the show grounds to wave our little paper Union Jacks. Early on we were completely immersed in Maori culture. Our family played music at the Maori club and at the tangis, and somehow that English culture was superimposed on what was really happening in the neighbourhood.

"Around the time I first went to school the hills all around Taumaranui were studded with freshly cut tree stumps, and the steam trains chugged up and down the main trunk line, their whistles echoing around the hills at night. On summer afternoons I used to ride my bike down by the river after school. The smell of honeysuckle was everywhere and it was truly beautiful. Then the local bullies would show up. They scared the crap out of me. I managed to side-step that stuff most of the time. I played guitar. It was my anchor. When it came my turn to be picked on, I'd just show them how to play the chord sequence of some song or other and suddenly we were all playing music instead of doing the whole violence thing.

"I have always been obsessed by music. At primary school all the other guys would be playing rugby and smashing at each other with hockey sticks and I would be hiding up a tree playing guitar. When I was really little I played ukulele – electric! – and Marc played along on pots and pans. One night when I was about seven I got a chance to play in my uncle's, Ed Turner's, band. It was such a great thing to play with other musicians and I guess that one night determined the course of my whole life."

Marc and Todd, 1960

Marc was two years younger than Todd and they were playing in a band from the time they started school. "We played at things like school socials and plugged our electric guitars into the old school movie projectors and turned them up full to get a great distorted sound."

When the Beatles arrived in New Zealand in 1964 there were very few television sets in Taumaranui. Todd and Marc and their friends were reduced to standing on the pavement outside the local electronics shop which had a TV on in the window. "Everybody gathered round the window at 6pm on a Sunday when the Beatles were due to be on. It was wild. There was no sound from the set, but even so there were girls screaming at the TV. We didn't know what it was but we knew it was something big. A few years later we saw *A Hard Day's Night* on a Saturday afternoon at the Regent picture theatre. It was completely thrilling and exotic. At the end of the movie the fire doors crashed open and all the kids poured out of the theatre and ran through the streets, screaming and shouting and singing those songs.

"The summer holidays would go on forever and we would take huge tyre tubes down to the Taringamoutu stream that ran through our place and float down to where it joined the Whanganui River. It would take us hours to get down stream to Taumaranui. We'd stop at lunchtime, walk into town and get fish and chips, and then we'd keep on going even further down river. In the late afternoon our father would come down after work and pick us up from the camping ground at Mananui. We would just spend the whole day on the river, singing and being stupid. Marc would sing at the top of his voice and the echoes would bounce off the cliffs. It was incredibly beautiful and idyllic in those days, and the river was very full. These days it has been dammed, and is mostly shallow rapids. Around the same time, guys who were the same age would go out with their rifles and shoot hundreds of goats off the side of a cliff, and rats down at the dump, so I guess our kind of fun was comparatively benign."

Because Todd and Marc were interested in music, Taumaranui was not altogether an ideal place in the world to be. "It seemed so far away from anything that was happening. We would read in *Time* magazine about Jimi Hendrix and the San Francisco scene and we knew that kids our own age were actually going to these concerts and not just reading about them. There was a lot of longing and mooning around because we were so far away from anything that was meaningful to us."

On Saturday nights the two boys would walk into town and meet their friends at the Taumaranui railway station waitingroom, which in the winter would have a fire burning. "At 11 o'clock the Auckland-Wellington express would come through, the cafeteria doors would bang open and people would get off the train to get a cup of tea. That was our entertainment. Sometimes Marc would get on the train and walk from one end to the other while it was stopped, stepping over sleeping bodies and talking to people who were awake. He would say that one time he was just going to stay on the train and get the hell out of Taumaranui.

"Marc and I were very close and very complicated. For instance, when we were at high school doing the dishes at night after dinner, there was a kind of psychological warfare that we would wage against each other. He would whistle in a demented tuneless way to annoy me. He would keep whistling until it drove me mad and I'd keep asking him to stop. In the end I'd hold up a plate and say, 'If you don't stop I'm going to drop this plate,' and he would just keep doing it with a crazed look in his eye. A few times I dropped the plate on the floor. As it crashed to pieces I'd yell out 'Sorry!!' to our parents who were elsewhere in the house, and Marc and I would be rigid with laughter. We used to goad each other unmercifully. We were sort of in it together somehow, we were closer than hell, but you couldn't

Todd singing, with Marc on drums, 1969

say that we were friends – it wasn't really that relaxed."

Todd sees his father, Stuart, as "a fantastic guy. Totally unpredictable. He would either be in a smouldering, black mood or he'd be laughing his explosive hysterical laugh. When we were very young our friends refused to come around and play with us because if he was home he'd say, 'Who are you?' in an abrupt manner, and they'd just scatter. They just didn't get the joke. Once, back in the '60s, I listened as he and his friends sat around talking. They were saying that what we need is a computer network where everyone can talk to each other. They were imagining the internet decades before it turned up. He got the first computer into local government in New Zealand, and it filled a large room. He would programme it using punch cards. There weren't even screens in those days. A team of guys came over from Canberra and invited him to come and work with them, but he turned them down. He poured his creativity into his job as the Taumaranui county clerk. The last two decades before he died in 1992 were a wonderful time to be around him. I loved it. I think the keenest part of the loss I felt for years after he died was the finality of not being able to talk to him anymore."

His mother, Voi, is still living in Taumaranui. Her father was part-Fijian and her mother from the King Country. She grew up in Fiji and went to school in Auckland during WW11, meeting Stuart just after the war when she was back in Fiji. She went over to Waitara by herself and stayed with his family until he got back from the Islands. "She's incredibly welcoming and generous, and when people meet her I know at some stage they are always going to say to me that they feel like they've known her forever."

After Todd left school he did a year at teachers' training college in Hamilton. Not long afterwards Dragon was formed, with Marc joining a few years later. "He was the wild man and I was the worried man. Marc would fill any room we played with his will and presence. His towering personality covered a huge range of the spectrum, and it was left to me to be the nice guy and pick up the pieces.

"When we toured America Marc would stride down the streets singing the songs about the cities we were in at the time – *24 Hours From Tulsa, New York, New York, I Left My Heart In San Fransisco*, and so on. His voice would boom off the buildings. Sometimes I'd tackle him and say, 'Why don't you just look around and see what's actually here instead of bending the world to your sound track?' and he'd say, 'Ah, ya righteous pussy, you just want everyone to like you.' He was probably right. The whole drugs and alcohol thing was too rugged for me, and when the deaths started it became totally overwhelming and menacing. It was all too real. I was everyone's older brother and it was intolerable to be cast in that role. In a rock band in the 1970s the worse you behaved the more you got rewarded for it. It was a wild anti-social experiment.

"Not long after we came over to Sydney in 1975, Marc's and my paths diverged. He got into a lot of stuff in Kings Cross that I knew nothing about. I would just hear vague rumours of dangerous wild living, and I didn't have the courage to find out what was really going on. In1977 I moved out of the band house and into a boarding house in Edgecliff to get away from the chaos. Slowly Marc and the rest of the band moved into the boarding house one by one. By the end, Paul Hewson was running the place while the ex-Nazi who owned it went away for a month. The lunatics were running the asylum! That was the place where Neil Storey died. When I drive past there now on the way to my kids' school I look at the grey office block that has been built on that site and think of all the mad things that went on there in the late '70s ...

"I was a complete catastrophist in those days. I would go into any situation, size it all up and ask myself what would be the worse thing that could happen here, and I'd have it sorted in my mind. Then something much more extreme than I could possibly imagine would happen.

"I was also the gatekeeper. When the debauchery was at its worst in the late '70s, I would ask for duplicate keys to our hotel rooms and every morning I would check around to see if everybody was still alive. Marc and I fought like dogs until we realised we were always coming to the same point from opposite directions. We struggled on until the band broke up for the first time on New Year's Eve in 1979.

"I went travelling around the world with my girlfriend, Johanna, who is now my wife. Before we left we arranged to meet Marc on the Spanish Steps in Rome at Easter. At the appointed time we were walking through a small laneway looking for our meeting place. Coming our way was a bearded, shaven-headed giant in knee-high boots and a huge denim jacket. The light was behind him and he was singing in Italian, his voice booming down the alley. Only when we were right next to him did we recognise Marc. He'd run out of money weeks before in Morocco and had been sleeping in parks and under bridges. He'd been to the New Zealand Consulate to get enough money to get back to Italy. He was a fabulous character, adrift in the world and completely happy. This was one of the few times that we were able to just be brothers."

In the 1980s Dragon re-formed and it became much more about the music. Even though "local area chaos" would occasionally take place, it was a more civilised time for Todd. But by 1995 he knew it was over for him. "I finally said to Marc, 'I've had enough now. How about I leave the band and we could just be brothers?' It was a much better arrangement. I moved away from Sydney, raised three sons and worked in a completely different area of music. Essentially, I made a new life for myself."

When Marc became ill in 1997, Todd had been doing the music for

Todd and Marc in Rome, 1980

the TV show *Heartbreak High* for four years. "I gritted my teeth and kept working through that whole horrible year. Marc went through hell, and his pain and suffering burnt away all the cynicism and all the things that tormented him. In the end he was transformed into the angelic guy that he had essentially always been underneath. He came down to the Shoalhaven NSW to die and is buried high on a hill overlooking the sea. There's a sense of peace in the graveyard that comes with the huge sweep of sky and sea. The week before he died we sat up there in the winter sun and he said that all he wanted was a little house by the sea. It was bitterly cold when he was buried and the wind was whipping at the Balinese flags by his grave. The church bells rang out over the boat harbour and there was a storm gathering over the sea. Some weeks later I sat by his grave and watched the whales on their way up the coast.

"Six months after Marc died, the world stopped for me and there was a vast silence. My life ground to a halt and I took a year off music to think about everything. It took that year and five years of psychotherapy to decode the meaning of my life. In a lot of ways that breakdown was Marc's greatest gift to me. It swept everything away with it and allowed me to start my life again without my grinding depression."

Around the time Todd organised Marc's grave, he reserved one for himself in the same cemetery. "Looking back, I think that maybe I was preparing to bury part of myself with Marc. His death was such a huge thing for me. I felt that life was very temporary. You look out from that graveyard over the Tasman Sea to New Zealand. In some small way it's what we've been doing for the last 30 years and it's comforting to know that we'll end up in the same neighbourhood."

Todd has travelled a lot over the years and seems to meet New Zealanders everywhere he's been in the world. "When I think of New Zealand there's a split thing in my mind. There's the sense of place and the people within it. On the one hand I see a powerful and beautiful landscape empty of figures and on the other hand I get a feeling about the New Zealand character and that Kiwi ingenuity which I've called on all my life. As a New Zealander you can always see a different way of making something work, or using tools or materials in a way that they are not supposed to be used. It works in music like that as well. You use

Todd Hunter

what's around you, sort of making do to survive, both physically and psychologically. I can't go back and live there as my life is too much embedded here, but in my heart I can only ever be a New Zealander.

"When I went back to New Zealand last time with the band I realised I was re-mapping my subconscious. I've had recurring dreams, over the last 20 years, set in the landscapes and houses I inhabited when I was young, and this time I went and visited a good number of them. Just to see these places again and check them against my subconscious was a very deep thing for me. We would arrive somewhere and I would check into the hotel then walk for three or four hours or drive out to places that had meaning for me. Places like the little Mount at Mt Maunganui, the cable car in Wellington, the guns by the Auckland Museum, looking out from a multi-storey building in Hamilton in the fog, walking along the river in Christchurch ... Scenes from recurring dreams made real.

"In New Zealand I find myself thinking about Marc a lot. With the re-emergence of the band I'm really feeling he's around. Had he been alive he would have kept the band going and I would have re-joined by now, so here I am. And no, I don't feel old up there. Being a musician you float above all that stuff, and it's a joy to get older. This is the fourth decade we've played. When we were playing in the St James Theatre in Wellington I looked out at a sea of 20-year-olds singing back at us and wondered how the hell they knew all the words of these songs that were around before they were born."

Also on one of his trips home recently Todd was encouraged to learn that the New Zealand government had finally recognised dyslexia. "As far as the Australian government is concerned, it doesn't exist! As a father of three creative and wonderful dyslexic boys, I'm very aware of the struggle involved. That's always been the side of New Zealand I love – people get active and change things for the better, and other countries follow. Hopefully they will on this one, too.

"In Australia we're in a huge landscape, and even though we're almost all crammed in along the East Coast there's anonymity to be found here. I find the closeness of New Zealand society a bit disconcerting. It's like a village on a country-wide scale. It seems as if everyone knows what you're doing and has a preconception about it. Where I live, two hours south of Sydney, it's very like the King Country. It's all big hills, dramatic cloud formations and running water. It's familiar, but different enough that I feel at home when I'm there in a way that I never did in Taumaranui.

"Recently in the early morning I walked the streets of Taumaranui with Johanna, and skipped stones down at the same river that I used to hang around at as a kid. We talked to a friendly old guy who was walking his dog and I had an acute sense of the life that I would have had if I'd stayed on in Taumaranui. The fog has finally cleared and it's so great to be able come back to New Zealand and see it clearly."

CHRISTINE 13 JEFFS

FILM DIRECTOR CHRISTINE JEFFS IS CONVINCED SHE SEES NOTHING MORE IN THE landscape of Aotearoa than the average New Zealander does. Her 2001 film *Rain* says otherwise. Speaking from her 120-acre property she shares with her partner, cinematographer John Toon, she constantly makes reference to the landscape, the nearby beaches and her assortment of beloved animals. Her love of New Zealand results in constant home-sickness while away filming, and an almost frantic need to return.

Needs must, however, as she spends months on end in America, filming and editing. Her compromise is doing as much work as possible in Los Angeles. "I'm closer to home if I'm on the West Coast," she says. "It would be good to make another New Zealand film, in fact there're a lot of films I'd like to do here. For instance there is the Otago landscape. I love that idea of the untamed New Zealand that the pioneers had to face – perhaps I'm thinking of my own family history.

"I grew up in Lower Hutt, up in the hills in Belmont. It was wild countryside. I could just walk across the road on to a farm, and there were always animals around. My whole childhood was running around outdoors. I think my education could have been better. I went to NaeNae Intermediate where some teachers would smoke in class." She vividly describes one. "He would smoke and talk at the same time – his lips would move loosely around the cigarette while it was jammed between his two front teeth."

Her greatgrandmother on her mother's side was a teacher who settled in the South Island. Those were the days when the school teacher was given a house in the country, which came with a cow. "It was pretty rugged and they lived a hand to mouth existence. My grandma wrote in her memoirs that on Christmas Day they would get an orange in the bottom of their Christmas stocking. It was the thing they waited for all year. She looked after all the kids while working for other families, doing washing and cleaning and even used newspapers for blankets."

Christine was encouraged to become a teacher herself, and applied for teachers' college. There was no film education then, so that wasn't a consideration. She was accepted, but decided not to go. Robin Laing gave Christine her first opportunity in the film industry by offering her the chance to become an assistant film editor. "I had been pottering around with various things in the video industry, but I wanted a job in film where I thought it would more exciting and artistic. I got into the editing and craft side of it. I did that for years and years and just loved it. I got to work with Gaylene Preston, Melanie Reed and John Laing. People

Christine Jeffs as a child

think of film-making more as a career now, but I don't think it was really considered that then. It was a bit fringe. There weren't any barriers that I would have taken on board. It would have been 'This is what I'm doing' and I wouldn't have thought twice about it. When I went into directing I felt I had lots of encouragement, and I was kind of single-minded about it.

"I suppose to be a director you have to be a little bit like a school teacher – you have to be all kinds of things. John sometimes says, 'You're not the director now!' Apparently I go into that mode quite easily. It hasn't really been in my nature, well, I didn't think so. I like to think I work in tandem with the producers and my creative team, and I love to hear people's ideas. I like to have strong collaborators. At the end of the day you have to make it work, and stand by the results."

Christine asks herself constantly whether she can have a career as a film-maker while staying in New Zealand "I think it would be very hard to work only in New Zealand unless you are like Peter Jackson and have already strongly established yourself as an international film-maker. Definitely I have films I want to make in New Zealand, but not all the films I want to make are New Zealand stories. John is the same – he works a lot overseas. I think it is a world-wide film community and you gravitate to like-minded people wherever you are.

"I think that coming from New Zealand we may bring a slightly different eye to how we see the world."

Recently she had discussions with the New Zealand Film Commission over what is a New Zealand film-maker and what is a New Zealand film. It appears it is an ongoing soul-search. "There's a film I want to do here that is an American story, but I don't consider it to be an American film. I want to do it as a New Zealand film-maker, and I want to bring my particular vision to it.

"So how do you define what New Zealand identity is, and how do you define what a New Zealand film is? How much is the vision of the film-maker got to do with making it a New Zealand film? How do you define what New Zealand identity is and how do you define what a New Zealand film is? These are all big questions and it's something that we are really grappling with. One of the big questions is how would New

Zealanders identify with it – would they claim it as a New Zealand film? That's got to do with lots of intangible things, such as the marketing and whether people will go, 'Hey that's our film-maker!' It's a catch 22 in so many ways.

"I consider myself a New Zealand film-maker who has a particular way of doing things – something that's come out of our number eight wire attitude, which is hands-on, working with the craft area of film-making, and then deciding to make a film. We have a way of doing things that is pioneering, I guess. I have noticed that there are more formalities in the way people make films overseas. Kiwis seem to expect good results from a more informal approach. Everything is more unionised in America and people have a strong sense of what is their exact role, especially crew. A lot of film-makers from New Zealand learn on the job. In America for example they seem to be more academic. Most of the interns I've met have a master's degree in film.

She thinks it's very important for any film she makes to have a sense of place that comes strongly from being a New Zealander and what is

Working as a film director

specific about the stories she wants to tell here in terms of the relationship between the landscape and the people. "For myself I like things to be real but not boring, and I like things to be funny. I'm asking the questions: What is the world that these people live in? What's outside the houses and what's the landscape? Maybe that's important to all film-makers. What I did with *Rain* was bring the exterior into the interior, and it's the same thing I'm trying to do with the film I'm working on now. I want to shoot the film for real – where you can see what's outdoors. See what really goes on and how it informs the characters.

"We shot *Rain* just near my home. In fact some of the locations I found while riding my horse along the beach. It was pretty exciting for it to do so well and for people all around the world to get it. It was about a classic Kiwi summer. Those baches don't exist any more – that area has been turned into a regional park. I'm very hopeful I'll be able to film something I've written again soon."

"Do I get homesick? Oh God yes, I hate going away, I never want to go. I don't like travelling at all. I don't want to miss the summer. I love it when the seasons change here. And I miss my animals so much.

"In America everyone drives everywhere and it's kind of a culture shock for me. Well, when you are in America stuck in a traffic jam on the 405 in Los Angeles, it doesn't seem real. I come back home to New Zealand every chance I get."

Christine feels New Zealanders can be a bit dour at times compared with Americans who, she says, are mostly bright and breezy. She finds that refreshing. "We are a bit down-in-the-mouth about things. It's like the taxi driver that picked us up from Auckland airport recently – he had his shorts tucked up around his waist and he sort of grunted at us, and then he marched ahead of us while we stumbled after him with our luggage. You know, that's the Kiwi thing. We don't talk things up like the Americans do. Such as the taxi driver – he doesn't say anything to make you feel good when you fly into the country.

"When you are in America no one mentions that, say, the Leader of the Opposition in New Zealand has resigned. You just don't hear of anything much to do with New Zealand. When John and I are working there we look up the New Zealand weather on the internet. John says,

'It looks like there's rain coming – it's going to be wet for a few days.' All he's worried about is if the grass is growing in Auckland. It's bizarre, don't you think? We take all our New Zealandness away with us when we work. We get a lot of comments from the crew about how they love Kiwis and have worked with Kiwis before, and that we have such a different way of working.

"I'm very glad I chose to do what I'm doing – talk about lucky! We have a very privileged life that we can go and live in another city and see what it's like. And working there feels different from being a tourist. You really get to feel the place."

John Toon works with other directors but he came to America with Christine to shoot *Sunshine Cleaning* which she directed. He's always her

Chris and John on the farm

Christine Jeffs

first choice as a cinematographer. They have worked together for quite a long time now, having met when he shot a short film for her in 1994. He works a lot overseas as he often shoots commercials, but he likes to be home, too.

The over-regulation of New Zealand Christine finds curious. "You can't even take your dog on the beach at certain hours, and we are a rural country. I think that's pretty weird. They don't seem to have problems in Hyde Park in London, but in New Zealand you can't even take them to the beach at certain times of the year, even on a lead. I thought we were a do-it-yourself kind of place. Now they are talking about bringing in restrictions on who can build your house. My dad built the house I was brought up in. That's what Kiwis did, build a room and then attach another room when needed.

"When talking about New Zealand Americans often say, 'Oh it sounds like a really beautiful place – we've always intended to go down there.' They just think it's some big park – they say they have a cousin who walked some track and said it was fantastic. It's totally about the outdoors. Quite often they think it is part of Australia – but lets just keep it a secret."

14

SAM NEILL

AFTER MANY YEARS LIVING AND WORKING OVERSEAS, 10 YEARS AGO SAM NEILL has finally settled back down in New Zealand. While he worries about the homogenisation of the rest of the world he is fiercely protective of his own country's future.

Sam has thought long and hard about his own New Zealand identity. But first there is something he would like to get off his chest.

"The most important thing about all of this is I don't see myself as a Kiwi. I am a New Zealander," he says with a wry grin. "Here people talk about good old Kiwi this and good old Kiwi that – it sets my teeth on edge. Those were not Kiwis who got off the boat at Gallipoli, and I don't see Ed Hillary as a Kiwi – it was a New Zealander who stood at the top of Mt Everest. It's like Aussie in Australia. If I was an Australian, I couldn't stand to be called an Aussie. When I think of Aussies and Kiwis, I think of those sad backpackers in London or Prague whose idea of a good time is to go to a pub and hang out with South Africans and other Aussies and Kiwis – it's pathetic! You know, I shake my head.

"There's something, too, about the word that's kitsch and cute, and that's not what we are. I see us as being people who stand tall in a new land. If people call me Kiwi, I tell them to get lost. There's nothing very cute about Aussie anymore. I associate that with the riots they had in Cronulla. The word is forever tainted with nationalism, narrow-mindedness and racism. They tried to drum up a bit of that during the America's Cup. I think it's plain embarrassing. I don't mind if people put a little Kiwi emblem on their lapels, but I'd sooner see a silver fern."

Warming to the question of who we are, Sam talks of the importance of having a clear acknowledgement of our geographical position in the Pacific. "There may be a few white people in the hills of the South Island who don't know who we are, but I think we are increasingly coming to understand that we are the capital of the Pacific. We are aware of how important Polynesian culture is to how we live and how we think, whether it is Polynesian or Maori. It's one of the things that make us different, and I value this. Auckland is a Polynesian city and, for all its problems, in a global sense these are pretty miniscule. But also I think we are moving beyond the bi-cultural thing, and we're becoming a more multicultural society.

"My own family is part-Asian and part-Maori and I think we're typical of many families in New Zealand. We've seen a big influx of Pacific Islanders into the country. We're looking at the second and third generation who are contributing an immense amount. Now we are seeing the same thing with various Asian people. It was pretty mono-cultural when I was growing up here. Quite dull, when you think about it. I'm actually very encouraged about our future in terms of our race relations, as compared with Australia. Don't get me wrong, I think there are plenty

Sam Neill at Mullaghmore House, Omagh, Co Tyrone, 1947

132

of terrific things about Australia. I've spent quite a bit of time there over the years, but I don't think their race relations have been addressed well at all.

"On the whole, the Waitangi settlements with the tribes haven't been without a certain amount of pain, but it has been good for the country. It's constantly evolving. You hear people complaining about the government giving away this and that, but actually what's been given away in terms of settlement is only a few years' profit from Telecom. If people come to me and talk about Maori bludgers, I won't wear a bar of it. The most important change the settlements have brought about is a whole new respect for Maori culture. It's central to the whole idea of New Zealand and what being a New Zealander is."

Sam Neill is a fourth-generation New Zealander who was born in the UK. His father was born in New Zealand, but was sent to school in England and went on to a career in the British Army, retiring around the age of 40. He then brought his family back to live in New Zealand. "This was in the mid-fifties and I was about seven at the time. My father, in common with many people of his generation, still referred to the UK as home. Although I was born there and I've lived there for several years in the early part of my career, it's never been home to me, neither in a literal nor a figurative sense. When we were coming out here my father talked about coming back to New Zealand – he never used the word home. My mother was English. I think she was probably homesick from time to time, but she was very stoic and never complained about anything. "My father was ambivalent about New Zealand. There were things that used to drive him mad and there were things that he treasured and loved about this place above all others.

We would head to the mountains in the holidays where he taught us to fish – we loved all that and I still do. He thought Central Otago, and the back of Canterbury, were as close to heaven as you could find on earth. But among the things that drove him crazy was the New Zealand accent. If there was a news reader with a strong accent, he'd shout abuse at the television screen. He liked, best, the way Maori people speak, with nice round vowels. The words don't come through the nose. They come from the stomach."

"I have to say I get flack for talking posh in New Zealand, but I don't think I have a posh accent. When I go to Europe I get a lot of flack from my friends for sounding colonial. There are certain New Zealand accents that I also find pretty difficult. I like the broad Australian accent. I find it very appealing – it has openness about it. There are certain New Zealand accents that are so pinched and nasal it sounds as if the speakers have a cold."

He had a couple of years in state schools when they arrived, and thereafter went to private schools. Whether or not that was a lucky thing he has no idea. "I do know that my parents sacrificed a lot to send us to private schools so I'm grateful for that. I suppose they were schools of their time, also slightly archaic. I was boarding from the age of nine – I don't know if that was lucky or not, either. If nothing else, I learnt to look after myself and eventually learnt about the things that I did like, like drama and debating. These were all extra-curricular and rather frowned upon. They were slightly poncy, but I think I and a few mates helped to

Brothers Sam and Michael, Christchurch, 1957

134

make them cool. I wasn't ever going to represent Canterbury at rugby – that was never going to happen."

He agrees it's true to some extent that wanting to be an actor in New Zealand in the early '70s was difficult because the film industry was so small. "There were a dozen actors in New Zealand who could make a living from acting at that time. I'd never heard of any New Zealander who was working in film. Secretly I wanted to work in the movies, but at the time it was so unlikely, that it wasn't worth mentioning. For people slightly older than me there were two scholarships a year. They would send actors to RADA, the Royal Academy of Dramatic Art, in London. People younger than me were able to go to drama school in Auckland. But they'd stopped the overseas thing when I came along and they hadn't started the drama schools yet, so for me there was no training to be had. So instead of doing what I should have been doing, getting my acting career up and running, I got a job as a film director at the National Film Unit. I stumbled into my film career rather unwittingly by a series of accidents. I did *Sleeping Dogs* and then I sat around for another year and a half doing documentaries because there wasn't going to be anything else coming up. *Sleeping Dogs* eventually led me to Australia It was really working over there that got me going in terms of a career. I thought when I did *Sleeping Dogs* that would be it, and it would have been if I'd stayed.

"I lived away for 20 years. Eventually I decided I wanted to come back to New Zealand. I'd built a house here 15 years ago. and always came for holidays, and eventually it occurred to me I wanted to live here permanently. If my career was everything, it would be better if I was living somewhere else, to be brutally honest, but my priorities are different now. Now I live here and I go away only if I have to. I think that is what we are good at, we are good at going away, and we are good at coming back We live in a very isolated corner of the world and it is necessary to travel and to open your eyes. You can't expect the world to come to you. So, carbon credits aside, I really do enjoy getting on an airplane and going somewhere interesting."

Sam explains he wears his identity with considerable pride when overseas, but at the same time he is loath to skite about it. "I don't think we can ever afford to be smug about New Zealand. The greatest thing we have going for us is also the worst. Our isolation is what will sustain us, but it is both a bonus and a trap. Psychological isolation is something we need to consider all the time, but physical isolation is going to be increasingly challenging for us. Now when I go to Europe people talk about not buying stuff from us because it has travelled 12,000 miles. It's now that we have to be smarter and greener and quicker than anyone else on the planet.

"New Zealanders like to think they are the best at a lot of things, and we're not actually – we're really good at some things, but we're not the best at anything much. On a good day, we play better rugby than anyone else in the world I get a great kick out of that, I love the All Blacks and I'll be at the World Cup, but let's not say it too loud because there are not too many people who care. The truth is there are a few white South Africans, and one or two people from New South Wales and Queensland, and a few home county poms and that's about it. The rest of the world is entirely indifferent to rugby. This might come as a shock if you live in Taumarunui.

"But what else are we best at? There are higher mountains here than anywhere else in the world. There are more hot springs here than in Japan, but Lemon & Paeroa isn't the best soft drink available in the world. The old route to survival was to think of yourself as a part of an empire or as America's friend. We know now – and this is an important point – we know now that that way madness lies. When you think of the standard of the current leadership in Australia, America and the UK, if we had blindly gone where they had wanted us to go five or so years ago, we would be in Iraq. Think of Iraq for a minute. The Americans went in there initially because of some response to 9/11. It was the war on terror, and now we know there was no connection between Iraq and 9/11. Then it was weapons of mass destruction. We now know there were none. Now it just seems they're in Iraq because of some strange ideological struggle.

"No, I believe very strongly that we need as New Zealanders to keep religion out of politics, and we need to be very careful we don't get caught up in that kind of madness. It's very important to see ourselves as part of the Pacific, friendly but independent – this bellicose madness has nothing

Sam Neill

to do with us. I don't like getting involved in politics at all, and I don't belong to any political party, but I did stand up and support Helen Clark's government because they have been very brave and sensible and God bless them for that. It was clear that Don Brash and his lot would have put us back into the American camp in the blink of an eye. There are many things about America that I like immensely, and I don't see myself as being anti-American, but I do have a great deal of anxiety about American leadership at present."

Sam readily admits he suffers from homesickness. He misses his family and his dog, but he also misses the country. Nevertheless when he is travelling he's never inclined to compare New Zealand with the country he's in. "Oh no, I never say, oh, it's better than this at home. That would be sad. And I don't go and drink with Kiwis in Kiwi pubs! I always make the most of where I am. It's the differences that I enjoy. And I do think the increasing homogenisation of cultures in the world is to be resisted. You can go to a shopping centre in South Africa or Bristol or Los Angeles and they all look the same – it's all so boring. You know there are so many things about Australians that are different from us and I enjoy that when I'm there, I don't regard it as a threat – it's something that I think is fantastic. We all have a chuckle about England, but there are certain things that are fantastically good about the place. Look at London. It's an amazing city."

He's alert to New Zealand's political vulnerabilities. "There are certain tendencies from time to time that I think we have to be vigilant about it. The country lurches to the right sometimes and produces people like Muldoon. Generally we're a progressive country, a liberal and compassionate place. But, having said that, there is always the chance of a backlash, and you see that when politics and the social milieu respond on occasion. I thought the whole Muldoon phenomenon was terrible. That was part of the reason I was pleased to get out of New Zealand when I did in 1978. I thought the country was going backwards pretty

Sam at his Otago winery

fast. Then I thought the whole asset-stripping of the country was very retrograde.

"In some ways New Zealand is a better place now – things have freed up a bit, apart from this occupational health and safety thing which has gone mad. The privatisation of New Zealand was rampant greed and in many cases it deprived us of our heritage. People get worried about Americans buying farms. It doesn't worry me at all – they can't take the farm back to Kansas. As long we ensure access to rivers and mountain tops, I don't think there is anything wrong with it We're allowed to buy land in America or England, so why can't they buy land here? I'm in no way concerned about that. Mostly wealthy Americans – I'm generalising now – will be better custodians of the land than one of us who wants to split it up and make a fortune."

Sam has noted, as others have, that it is quite common for ex-pats to come back to New Zealand, especially if they've done well, to face that attitude of 'Who do you think you are?' Or even worse, 'If you're so smart what are you doing here?' He notes that this says so much about what such people think of their own place.

The only dark side he himself can see in New Zealand is in the bush which early Europeans were keen to cut t down as it appeared too dark and foreboding. "It was scary and spooky – there might have been dangerous natives in there somewhere. We don't have a great custodial history in this country, and a lot of the land has been thoroughly exploited. It's still going on today, but all I can say is thank God for national parks."

But what he mostly wants to say is how he feels when he returns to New Zealand.

"I don't really think of myself as home until I get off the plane at Queenstown. The most exhilarating thing to do is to breathe in a big lungful of air. I do a big 360 degrees around the mountains and I get a rush of endorphins. I'm home."

KERRY FOX

ACTOR KERRY LIVES IN LONDON WITH HER HUSBAND ALEXANDER LINKLATER, an award-winning journalist, and their two children, "Being a New Zealander is a big part of my identity. It's completely about the way I live, the way I set up my life".

Of the 34 film and TV productions Kerry Fox has appeared in, *An Angel At My Table*, 1990, and *Intimacy*, 2001, are the best known, particularly the much lauded *Intimacy*, a bleak, sexually explicit film. She has been offered many roles in the UK, but she has two young children, so at present she is more defined by being a mother than by being an actor. As for the future, "I can't say I'll be working in a year's time. I might get no work at all – it's not unheard of. But I've never been in the position to say what I'll be doing in six months' time," Kerry says.

In spite of her early success in New Zealand, Kerry feels she would have difficulty slotting back into the industry here. "If I came back I would have to relinquish my career, without a doubt. I'd have to do something else." Nor could her husband do what he's doing now.

But inevitably this leads to the nature of the New Zealand film industry and its wanting bankable stars in its projects. "You look at some of the films made here with any money. They don't use New Zealand leads. They just need people with bigger names." Kerry doesn't feel this is solely because of the financial backers of a project. "The people making the movies want to work with these types of people, stars. So it's not entirely industry finance-led. My friends acting in New Zealand find it difficult.

It's a real struggle for them, and I would be in the same situation if I moved back."

Like most ex-pats Kerry says that keeping in touch with other Kiwis is important to her. "There is a strong affiliation of New Zealanders in London in the sense that we stick together and support one another. I certainly don't feel anything other than a New Zealander, and I'm really proud of the others' successes, in arts and culture. But I also keep in close contact with my friends at home. We talk constantly on the phone, people I get along with so well, and I make those connections with Australians too. The English are particularly hard to befriend. I can speak only from my own experience but I've always found they try to pigeonhole and define you, and they find that very hard to do with New Zealanders.

"Kiwis work really hard and the English respect what they do, but people are also shocked. I've got a Kiwi girl working for me as a nanny for a couple of days a week and she is phenomenal. She does anything – she wraps the baby up against the cold and takes it out there while she's mowing the lawns. She does anything in the house that needs to be done. It's just amazing. My English friends have never seen anything like that before in their lives. They just can't relate to it. They like to know what class people are in, so they know how to treat them. When I first started in England, being a Kiwi was a great advantage because I felt I could knock on anyone's door and use that first two minutes before they realised who I was, and glean as much as I could, whereas English people just won't cold-call. I think we are special in that way," and she laughs.

Kerry grew up in Lower Hutt in the 1970s, in a world far removed from her life today. Back then she never dreamed of going out in the world to seek her fortune. "Oh no, that wasn't what I was thinking. In fact I never thought of leaving New Zealand. I didn't see that as part of my future at all."

She doesn't feel that the education system nurtures ambitions along those lines. "Unlike today, there was little pressure back then to do well or strike out. You were expected to get high marks, but I didn't find that difficult, and you were expected to go on to university, and I did. In fact, I went twice, the first time to Victoria University, but I hated it. I found it a very lonely place. I had all these images of its being full of

Kerry Fox in her garden

incredibly articulate and exciting people having amazing conversations about politics and art at lunchtimes – and there was none of that at all. I didn't find it inspiring in any way. I even felt that what I was learning in lectures was nothing new. I just couldn't deal with it."

Kerry's next venture into tertiary education was shaped by one particular teacher. "My biggest influence was learning speech and drama from this teacher, Heather Salmon, who taught me for at least 15 years. She was phenomenal, and really drew out of me a lot of the qualities that I live on now. The most important thing she taught me was being able to listen and encourage other people to put out the best of their ideas, and to show that their ideas are welcome. From her I realised I'd always known I wanted to be an actor, but it never seemed a realistic choice. And I didn't want to apply for drama school because my sister had applied . . . well, she had an application form. But in the end I think I applied twice!"

During the 1980s Wellington had quite a good theatre community with a number of small venues providing work opportunities for young actors, so she took a gamble on drama school. "Once I had decided to be an actor, and got into the New Zealand Drama School in Wellington, after trying varsity, it was a huge, huge, change in my life, probably the biggest. But I imagined my future as just being an actress in New Zealand. I was very committed to the development of the New Zealand culture and the New Zealand voice. There was no concept of being a film actor. It was going to be theatre or what was available on TV. I never thought of leaving to work away from home." She did some work for Bats Theatre and the Depot Theatre, and sometimes operated lights. This occupied about a year until she was cast in *An Angel at My Table*. This role of Janet Frame was pivotal for Kerry's career, and working with Jane Campion opened up many possibilities. But the realisation that she was creating a role of a living person was daunting. "I didn't know what I was stepping into, really. I didn't have a real impression of Janet Frame. I knew some of her poetry, but I hadn't read much of her prose.

"But Jane Campion is an extraordinary director. She was able to deliver her best in that situation, and take us with her. The only restrictions were the obvious tight financial restrictions on that film, which was amazing. Jane was very well supported by everyone around her, and the wonderful script made it all come together.

"I think everyone who was involved was, to a certain extent, naive. That is a great quality of New Zealanders. All the naiveté leads to a bravado that carries you a long way – you've got nothing to lose. You can throw yourself into it without hesitation, and great things can be achieved. The whole experience of doing that film completely changed my life in so many ways. It really set its direction as well, I think. It gave me many opportunities. But I didn't get any film offers after it came out. Nobody wanted to employ a fat girl in a cardigan! However I didn't have to prove to anybody that I could act. The world opened up to me. I travelled for the first time because of that film. People respected it and what I'd done, and in many ways it literally opened doors."

Kerry left New Zealand to make the most of those open doors. "Acting is so much about luck, having the opportunity – which you can create for yourself – and being able to make the most of the opportunity, being ready to do your best when the opportunity arises. I don't think it just lands in your lap, certainly not for me. I created as many opportunities as I could for myself from that one stepping stone. I worked really hard to put all my energy and focus into travelling and trying to find opportunities for my life, and also being ready to do the best I could should an opportunity come up. But it didn't come up for about a year, so it was a terrible struggle. There was a period of waiting for the film to come out, and then there was a long time tracking people down and hassling them about possible work, whether it was in America or in the UK. I moved to Sydney and even there I had to prove myself before anyone would employ me."

The alternative to moving overseas would have been to stay in New Zealand and work in TV. But Kerry is "not that sort of actor. I don't think my specific qualities at that stage were for soap opera or 'fast run-around' TV. I was smart enough to realise that I wasn't going to be appreciated in that environment. I can't work it. I'm not very good at it. I think it is a specific skill and it's not a skill that I have. I do think it's a special talent. Since *An Angel at My Table* the only other film I have done in New Zealand is *The Last Tattoo,* but it never really screened anywhere, and I've also done a film about the *Rainbow Warrior* bombing."

Working and living overseas has influenced the way she views New Zealand and its political landscape. "Apart from some of the politics being a bit 'dodgy', I think New Zealand is pretty impressive. Its financial model is one of the world's leading models – the fact that farmers don't have any subsides, that's something virtually unheard of anywhere else. People seem to have a political comprehension that doesn't necessarily occur in the rest of the world. Because New Zealand is so isolated there is an unworldliness sometimes it appears very separate from the rest of the world, away from its impact.

"The race riots in France recently wouldn't have had any impact. I think we should take notice of what's happening with other country's cultural struggles, and then maybe we would learn at lot more. New Zealand has been battling with its own multiculturalism and assimilation issues for so long that it's constantly redefining the issues. Maybe we are just concentrating on making it work here and we're not connecting any of our problems with what's happening in other countries."

Kerry agreed that New Zealander's wouldn't wrap themselves in their national flag, as some Australians did during their racial troubles in 2006. "That seems to be such an American thing to do. Because the Maori and Islander population is so strong and widespread, it's diluted that passion for power and success and single-minded greed that runs through a lot of modern white societies. Americans have that terrible rise of fundamentalism, and the American dream that everyone has the right to what they want.

"I come from the tradition of our drama school headteacher. He showed us that we could never be *expected* to be employed, and it was entirely up to us what we made of our careers and our culture. He made us feel that we had a responsibility to our culture. That has been so important to me."

In Kerry's experience there is a New Zealand attitude of 'You mustn't be too successful', 'You mustn't speak out' – the tall poppy syndrome. 'Success in New Zealand can mean you are leaving people behind and you're not taking part in your community. It's seen as negative. Success is a subjective thing, totally relative. It's seen as a success if you get a part in *Shortland Street,* for goodness sake! But to me success has to be something you define for yourself and you can achieve it for yourself only through risk. Opening yourself to risk also means opening yourself to failure, and success is just the by-product – it shouldn't be the goal."

Many New Zealanders feel that their long-term woman prime minister has been a role model for change. But Kerry has always seen New Zealand women as being strong. Rather than Helen Clark being a role model, Kerry wonders whether she is "merely representative of where New Zealand women are right now. You can see this in a reverse way – we have so many women in power because of the nature of our society. It's the end result of how New Zealand society functions that we have very strong women here. I'm always being asked why I myself choose to play strong women. What other women do I know? I don't know any weak women! I can't think of one woman I know who is weak. I think maybe Helen Clark is just a masthead for our society. The obvious conclusion is that we have a strong female contingent in power in government, which is great. I see it as a good thing for New Zealand. It's one of the feelings you have when you return, that you're coming back to a very positive country. Maybe I just take it for granted. How do I say this? It's just the way that I was brought up I suppose."

Even after so many years of living in England, Kerry strongly identifies with being a New Zealander. "It has really formed who I am. There is a sense of adventure and openness about us, and people respect us for that. In England there is a kind of colonialist attitude of looking down on us but that is the case with any country that thinks that what they have to offer makes them superior. It's human nature isn't it? Being a New Zealander is seen in every aspect of my life. Take my house. I try to make it like a New Zealand patch in the middle of London. I have a huge kitchen with a sunroom out the back with a eucalyptus tree – I know it's Australian, but it's close enough. I've just planted a ponga and a cabbage tree, and I have toi toi and kowhai. Whenever I hear anyone from home is coming to town and they don't know anyone, I have them over. My husband Alex who is a Scot calls all this the 'Kiwi Kabal'. He secretly likes it because Kiwis are interesting and well travelled and open to experiences."

Kerry doesn't like that white ex-pat thing "where parents give their children Maori names", but her interest in the language has increased. "People in New Zealand are now using Maori words that I don't even know. It just makes me realise I've been away for 15 years and how it's all changing so much. People seem to fall into the Maori language. They say 'Kia ora' so easily. Language mutates, I guess. I've found that I pronounce Maori words differently each time I return. When I got married I found a Maori poem and it was so appropriate that I felt I had to read it during the ceremony. I worked really hard to pronounce the words properly. It's the same for my husband, too. We tell our son he's Scottish as well as Kiwi, and we fight really hard for this."

An Angel at My Table quickly had a huge impact on an audience who wouldn't have known much about Janet Frame's work until then. It sparked an interest in her books. Had this influenced her decision to take on the role? "There were probably a lot of people who didn't know her, and the movie made her books more popular. People began reading her which I think is great. What the movie did for me was crediting me with intelligence, which is really nice. Actresses aren't really considered

Kerry Fox "credited with intelligence"

intelligent. Since my marriage I've have moved into the journalistic world, and I am so aware of how differently they are treated. It's mind-boggling. I remember going to a newspaper lunch and sitting with an editor, and some other actors were there, really interesting people. In the past, the actors were treated off to the side, but the editor had so much respect for Alex's magazine – *Prospect*, a political-cultural essay monthly – and my father-in-law is also a really well-respected UK journalist. It means when I'm out there I can see myself as an intelligent political person which I really enjoy. I lean on it now."

Like most actors, Kerry is well aware that to stay in the game she has to be persistent. "Oh, definitely. An actor's career is a rollercoaster and you have to recognise that's the way it is. There is no security and you might have massive ups and downs for three months or you might be in

147

a pit for three years. A very tiny minority of actors do have a continuous stream of work. For some people who have become famous, it hasn't fallen from the sky. It's something they have really wanted and they have been very, very, driven to achieve it and have committed their whole life to it. A huge amount of energy is needed to be a star, but I'm not a star and therefore I feel I've got limited choices."

Kerry will not elaborate on which films she had to pass on and now regrets the decision. "No, no, I can't!" The movie *Intimacy* has had the most impact on the direction of her career, although she fears some people might be frightened about working with her. "Every role you do stays with you slightly. It depends on who you are working with, and who the director is or whether they can accept stuff from you. It affects who you are. When I had success with *Intimacy*, the pride I had in the things people wrote to me from New Zealand was just phenomenal. It was amazing, really moving. These were people I didn't even know! It was really great that people were proud of it. I thought it was a very truthful movie. It was just that it wasn't romantic, and some people thought it depressing."

I'm surprised that there were negative repercussions to that role, such as other directors' attitudes towards working with her. "It was huge, it meant that no director wants to touch me, absolutely. Undoubtedly, people are terrified to work with me anyway. Lots of directors want to know what they are getting, they want to be reassured. They aren't particularly adventurous, they aren't open to discovering anything new, and they just want an actor to deliver. I'd work with the director of *Intimacy* again, we are really close friends, but I don't think it will happen. I probably won't work with Jane Campion again, either. Some films are too hard, they cost so much of your secret life. It's not limitless. It's too scary. *Intimacy* was the best thing I've ever done, undoubtedly. I'm so pleased I did it, but there are consequences from doing this kind of film. I don't get scripts. I'm aware a lot of scripts just don't get to me – you know, agents aren't just people who get you work. They do deals."

I wondered whether that has anything to do more with her being a New Zealander. Many of us find our sense of humour is misunderstood overseas. Did Kerry find that? "Yeah, I'm lot more careful now. I find there are so many people who don't understand my Kiwi humour, and I've become more pedantic about my language, which may or may not be a good trait. I have to be careful I don't alienate people with the way I respond to them. I'd hate to do it to people. I do temper my New Zealand-ness – unless I want to get a rise out of someone!"

ROGER DONALDSON

ROGER DONALDSON IS AN INTERLOPER, WORSE STILL AN AUSTRALIAN. HE ARRIVED in New Zealand in 1965 after spending the first 19 years of his life in Ballarat, Victoria. Instantly he fell under the country's spell. After years of film-making in New Zealand, including *The World's Fastest Indian*, he has shown he most certainly understands the New Zealand psyche.

Speaking from Australia, he reiterates his love affair with the country. "If someone asks where I come from, I just say I was born in Australia but I became a film-maker in New Zealand and was involved in the formation of its film industry. All my kids are New Zealanders, and I just love the place."

Roger studied geology in Ballarat for a year. Then he decided to take a year off, and, with another student friend, Gorol Dimo, headed to New Zealand – an easy trip to make, with no passport or reason needed. "I had a bit of wanderlust, and this, combined with the feeling that I didn't want to carry on doing geology, was enough for me to begin searching for something else to do. But I did have an interest in the arts, so I guess I was a rather confused 19-year-old. It also looked as if I was going to be drafted to Vietnam, so I needed time to think about what was going to happen on that front.

"Before we left we had arranged jobs, working on the Manipouri Power project as geologists, and somehow they had it in their heads we were coming for three years. But we'd planned to be there for only three months, so they said, 'There's no job for you – we don't want you for such a short time.' We had been hitchhiking south and had arrived there with only a one-way ticket, the plan being to earn our money for our ticket home. So there we were, suddenly in Invercargill, and with no money. Where could we go?

"We heard there was hop-picking to be done in Nelson, and they'd just opened the Haast Pass that week so we hitched to Nelson to get jobs. Unfortunately we arrived there just before Christmas, and no one wanted to hire anyone then because they would have had to give them holiday pay. My mate said he was going to work in a pine plantation, but I decided to stay in the bright lights of Nelson. I got a job as a beach photographer, my first job in the world in photography. But it wasn't very lucrative. I think I earned 13 shillings and 6 pence in two weeks which wasn't even enough to pay the rent. As good fortune had it, I met a very accommodating Kiwi girl who invited me to come and stay with her and her parents. Once settled I got a job in Harley's brewery, knocking the corks into the top of flagons. By that time I had fallen in love with New Zealand and decided to stay."

Roger had been looking for something different when he arrived, and he says that's exactly what he found. "And it's still like that for me. At

Gorol Dimo and Roger Donaldson hitchhiking, 1965

151

the time I don't remember running into too many Australians like myself, but I just loved the country. It was very friendly and it seemed a lot more down to earth than Australia was. Maybe it was just escaping from Australia and the life I had here, and just being a young guy on his own. I was discovering a new life, and in doing so I discovered myself. There's nothing like travelling to another country at that age without a backstop. Suddenly I could reinvent myself and be who I wanted to be, and not the person everyone else thought I should be.

"When I used to send photos back to Australia of New Zealand's snowy Alps, people would go, 'Oh my God, there is *snow* there?' They had no idea what New Zealand was like, which is funny when you think about it, because I still don't think Australians have an idea what it's like. If you were going overseas at that time, I suppose New Zealand was the first choice as it was so easy to get to. When I think about it now, it was England that I was trying to head for, but when I fell in love with New Zealand it didn't cross my mind to go any further."

Over the years his photography extended into film-making. Collaborating with Ian Mune, he made a number of small dramatic films which Roger says were the first New Zealand films to sell overseas. Among these were seven half-hour TV films called *Winners and Losers* which were sold to 52 countries. "This was back in the 1970s when there were people running television channels, such as the French, Germans and the Americans, who would be interested in buying films about New Zealand. We started off at a trade fair in Cannes and from there we went knocking on doors. The world had never seen any films from us before. They were also fascinated by New Zealand being a country that was at the end of the earth. I went on to make *Sleeping Dogs* in 1977, a film of the C.K. Stead novel. It was seen as a big and important step in the beginnings of the New Zealand film industry, and was the first colour film made there. So it was a unique film, and it had a big impact in New Zealand."

By the time *Sleeping Dogs* was made, Roger had been in New Zealand for 10 years. "I was a Kiwi by then," he says. "I was still trying to discover my own identity, and it was a very friendly down to earth place, and still is. Another advantage was that it was very different politically. For one thing it had a more relaxed policy on the Vietnam War than Australia

Roger (left) with Ian Mune

did. It had some troops in Vietnam, but it didn't have conscription.

"I didn't go back to Australia for a visit for seven years. I guess I was getting homesick, but by then I had a wife and kids and I was well ensconced in New Zealand. Even now while I'm working in Australia, or any other part of the world, I still have a very strong connection to the country. I made *The World's Fastest Indian* there, and that was very much a New Zealand experience." Roger Donaldson has a vineyard in the South Island and a house in Auckland, and two of his children live in New Zealand. "It's still very much in my consciousness and in my life. When I first arrived there I found there was a naiveté I mean that in the best possible sense – of not having being exposed to the rest of the world, but while there is still some of that naiveté, Kiwis are probably the most well-travelled people in the world. It's a place you wouldn't ever want to turn your back on because it's so different from the rest of the world. You may not have so many opportunities, if, say you're interested in movie-making, or some of the things that take a bigger population to support them, but just to be there is a fantastic experience.

"What I love when I go there is how little distance you have to travel to see major changes in topography. It's visually a very stimulating place and the weather changes so dramatically. You put all that together, and you never forget it. You know, it starts at the airport – you can get a trolley and put your luggage on and you don't have to pay for it!"

When the subject of socialism in New Zealand comes up, Roger makes a point of referring to it as 'social responsibility'. "I see it as the back-bone of New Zealand, a fair go for everybody. Nobody wants to get rich – well, in my mind, anyway – on the back of anybody else. I've been more than happy to drive my fast cars and stuff like that, but I don't think it's every man for himself. It doesn't have the negativeness of a real socialist country, but it could end up eroded a bit as the world becomes more capitalist. I think New Zealand has always been a place for the disenfranchised and the less fortunate. And it's small enough for those things to be issues that can be handled. Not that it's not without its problems, but I think it's like a small village – if anybody does something bad you are often touched by it yourself.

"New Zealand was born of a brutal past and the Maori were never defeated. They've had a tough time, what with disease and coping with education, and just assimilating to a western way of life. I think it's been very hard for them, but on the other side of the coin there has been an assimilation of the races. Many people have now got some Maori blood if they've been there for several generations. Race is not a matter of black and white as it is in Australia. I think New Zealand is now becoming very proud of its English and Maori heritage. My first experience of meeting any Maori was within days of hitchhiking around the South Island. A car stopped and there were about eight Maori guys in this car and this one guy said, 'Hop in' and I said 'Where?' There were two of us needing a lift. He said, 'You just lie on top of us.' So we had to lie on top of them, and these guys were the greatest guys you could ever meet. That sold me on the Maori."

When he thinks of what happened in the Land Wars, and the complications of what followed, he sees stories of darkness, treachery and heroism, two completely different cultures meeting each other. "I've heard the stories of when one Maori tribe was looking as if they were going to beat the other side how it stopped and gave them some ammunition to keep the fight going. Those are the some of the great stories of New Zealand. I would love to do one of those in a film, but it might be a little hard if you're not Maori."

He says the New Zealanders he knows are the most active and on the ball people, but like anywhere he concedes there are some New Zealanders who 'sit back and smoke a doobie' and take it easy. "New Zealanders are tolerant of both sorts. You don't have to be a super achiever to feel there is a place for you, and you don't have to feel embarrassed if you want to bring home the America's Cup, either. Take Peter Jackson. I think New Zealanders on a whole are incredibly proud of what he has pulled off, and the fact that he managed to do it in New Zealand is even better. He has single-handedly changed the profile of the country. I think Peter is probably a version of Burt Munro, of just not seeing the obstacles, and then just believing in himself. He's a great inspiration. It would be mean-spirited if you had anything negative to say about him. I wish him only the best.

"I think New Zealand has always celebrated the odd. It is a place where the eccentric is a treasure rather than an embarrassment. You take the Prime Minister. She's not the sort of person you'd think would get elected, and when she was – what a breath of fresh air! She is unique. A very real politician, certainly, but what you would hope a politician would be, someone who believes in leadership. You certainly don't get the impression she got the job with some great lobbyists working for her. She got it because she wants to do something for the country. Women

Roger Donaldson with Diane Ladd and Anthony Hopkins

155

have been well represented in politics and the arts in New Zealand. Maybe it was hard for her being a woman, and maybe it wasn't. I would hope it wasn't."

Roger's Central Otago vineyard produces his 'Sleeping Dogs' wine label, and although he sells only in New Zealand he says he tries his best to make a good wine. "It's economically not easy to make wines there because you have to subsidise them, unless you're really on a big enough scale to reduce the prices. Also labour costs are high compared with the other countries you're competing against. It's not easy, but I feel people should also be happy to pay more for a local bottle of wine. There is a lot of pride in the fact that New Zealanders can make some world-class wines, and that's what we try to do."

As for the pool of sheep jokes that Australians have gathered over the years, he sees them as a perfectly natural occurrence. He can't resist one himself. "What do you call a Kiwi with five sheep? A bigamist!" and he laughs. "Jokes have always got a mean edge to them, and I'm not too sure if they are taking the mickey out of sheep or out of New Zealanders. Anyone who's been to New Zealand always says there's a lot of sheep, don't they?"

In Roger's opinion the only dark side New Zealand might have is the darkness one might find in the bush. "There can be quite a feeling of foreboding, but it's bush you can dive into and there's nothing there except for wetas. When I was first there, I'd see this dark and impenetrable bush and I was a bit intimidated by it, and then someone said, 'Well it's not like Australia. Just jump in and lie down and nothing is going to bite you!' I love that.

"I feel loyal to both New Zealand and Australia. I was born in Australia and can't claim I'm anything but Australian, but I have a real fondness for New Zealand. I love it, and I love being there. Most Australians who have never been there, even now, have no idea of just how diverse and how different it is from Australia. I think that, overall, New Zealand is a very independent country compared with Australia. They are about as far apart as you can get."

JON TOOGOOD

17

"My parents were British immigrants who grew up in London during the war. They were pretty much working-class. I mention this because, as a child growing up in Wellington, I could never really relate to the idea of being from or born into any particular 'class' at all," Jon Toogood says.

"My friends at school were from all over the place. Some were rich, some not so rich, Maori, Pakeha, Samoan, Cook Islander, Korean, Indian – whatever. I never felt there was any restriction on what I could choose to do with my life when the time came. I still feel that way and it makes me very happy that my folks decided to move to New Zealand and raise their family here. They have always been extremely supportive of anything I've done and I am very thankful for that."

Having travelled around the world as lead singer in Shihad, Jon has been exposed to many cultures. He is acutely aware, however, of where his allegiances lie – back in the country which gives him constant inspiration.

Jon's parents immigrated to New Zealand in 1958, and after returning to England briefly the couple married and decided in 1963 to make Wellington their permanent home. Growing up in a very English household, where the only 'relatives' around were other English immigrant friends of his parents, Jon enjoyed a raft of traditional English food including dripping on toast, "which I still eat – yeah, fat on toast! My mother being brought up in the war told me I had to eat it because it is the goodness in the meat, not realising it's the bad bit. I still love it!

I was the only kid at school with white sugar sandwiches. I have a very sweet tooth."

Warming to the subject he continues, "At school I was surrounded by Kiwi culture, but at home I was exposed to a lot of English music favourites. I distinctly remember songs like Peter Sellers' *Any Old Iron* and Tommy Steele's *Little White Bull*. Our house was often filled with British people getting together to remember the good old days. They all loved being in New Zealand but were proud of where they came from. I can imagine the isolation here could have been difficult and I think it was a pretty brave move to make." He says he's asked his parents about it over the years and they've said that London was becoming overcrowded and that New Zealand had fewer people and better air. "But they've never really talked about it that much." Could he imagine doing that himself? "I've been to some beautiful countries around the world which I love, but I would never consider packing up all of my belongings and going and living in another country – especially from here.

"I went to Island Bay Primary, and when anyone picked up a guitar to sing I would stop whatever I was doing. I couldn't think of anything

Jon with his favourite toy car as a child

else while I was listening to music. My other love was drawing and that's where my good marks came from."

While at Wellington High School Jon formed a band with some school mates. This was the band that evolved into Shihad. "The difference between us and some other bands was we had no intention of staying in New Zealand. We weren't planning to live anywhere else, but we wanted to tour everywhere, we wanted to be not just a good New Zealand band but a good rock band."

He goes on to explain that their enthusiasm was born out of naiveté. "We just wanted to go to any country in the world and play." Doing what almost every other aspiring Kiwi band before them had done, they started off with an Australian tour. Their first big move, however, was to Berlin where they got a record deal. "We thought, 'Yeah now we're a real band!' We had seen a couple of friends' bands go to Australia and then get lost because there is that Australian thing of 'We have our own rock bands here. We don't need another New Zealand band.' With us, touring just didn't stop. We toured through America and Europe for eight months and lived in Berlin and we had lucky breaks along the way. I love that life. I love going to new cities and seeing new places."

The biggest thing, he says, was that it made him appreciate where he was from. "When I come back to New Zealand, here the air is completely clear and everything appears in high definition – I don't know what it is, there is just something about the atmosphere here. It's so clear and pure and humbling, the landscape is humungous, and it really gives you a perspective on where you fit in with things."

Jon observes there is a definite melancholy in New Zealand, "which I love, and I've never been able to explain why it's like that." Thinking about it more, he says, "New Zealand is pretty up-to-date but it still has that isolation that we can't get past. And I think it has got something to do with sadness, and it's a sweet sadness to me. It's not a bad thing. I love it. It feels like reality to me. I'm more clear-headed here than anywhere else, and I find it very inspiring as far as creating goes. Just looking out my Wellington window here in Brooklyn, over to the mountains, hills and big harbour and the native bush – it is just beautiful."

The subject of earthquakes comes up. "When I was a kid I used to find earthquakes exhilarating, I'd be thinking maybe the school would be closed. Maybe I could go downtown and grab that TV or video game I want." He laughs. "A little bit of a crim, there. I've never looted in my life!" Having now done some reading about the subject he admits to being not so fearless. "But I don't dwell on it. I think you have to be hardy to live here. I'm a skinny wee thing and so I've always had to rug up in the winter. I like to put on layers of clothes and having a fire and keeping warm. When we were living in LA in the winter I couldn't tell the difference in seasons and I found it quite static and boring after a while. I enjoy the unpredictability of the weather here. Wellington looks different every day and I love that."

Asked to describe what he thinks of his countrymen, he doesn't hesitate. "We tend to observe before we bother opening our mouths. We first like to hear what other people have to say before we go putting our ideas on to anybody. I find it's best not to be judgemental. I'm not big on generalising. If I'd been asked this question when I was younger, I would have given a whole list. I've met so many different people from around New Zealand it's a very creative place. People think outside the square because we have the space to do so. We are removed enough from American and British culture. We've got enough isolation to create a culture of our own even though it still has major connections, and that's really cool.

"There's an element of straight up-ness that I find here, an accepting of other people's cultures that I don't think happens in Australia and America. I hate the word multi-cultural because it's bandied about in Australia too much. There is a lot they have to sort out because they are not dealing with it at all. I also think there's a lot to be sorted out over here between the Europeans and the Maori, but at least we have dialogue. A lot of my Australian friends can't believe we were taught Maori as a compulsory subject – well, why not? On my cigarette packet it's got 'Smoking Kills' and there's the Maori for 'Smoking Kills' as well, and on my passport half of it is in Maori. I think that's great, I'm so proud of that. But I hate people to gloat about it – I think it's just the way it should be. It's what makes us special and by embracing that we've given ourselves more depth as a culture and it makes us unique. My wife's father is Te

Ati Awa Maori and I've definitely learnt a lot about New Zealand culture from her side of the family."

When Shihad moved to Australia seven years ago, they were given an option about where to live. They chose Melbourne because it reminded them of home. "It's the most liberal city. New Zealand differs from city to city, but there seems to be quite a left-leaning bias. You even see the National Party playing the middle ground, and that's what they need to do to get the votes. As they've found out, the idea of letting

Jon Toogood

nuclear ships in made even the right-wing go 'Stuff that!' We're naturally inclined to go towards a left-thinking society, which I really like.

"There is more of a secular way of thinking in place in New Zealand. Being atheist is something I'm proud of but I don't consider myself non-spiritual. I think the universe is an amazingly wonderful place. Music and art make up my religion and that's where I get to experience my magic. There is a real spiritual side to New Zealand and you are constantly reminded of your place in the scheme of things. Wellington is surrounded by water and hills and you never ever get that feeling of humanity being above nature – at the very least you are a part of it all. I find it humbling in a good way."

Nonetheless Jon can feel a little removed at times, something which he puts down to being a musician and constantly entertaining people. He finds it more of a culture shock living in America than living in Europe. "There are more similarities to our culture in Europe. It's different in

Jon with his wife, Ronise Paul

Australia where there is more of a bias towards America. They don't like to hear that, of course – some of the most vicious rants about the subject I've heard come from Australians. Things are a lot louder and bigger and people are in your face – it's just full on. Whereas in Europe it is a little more – I don't want to sound wanky – but it's a little more reserved."

He feels at home when he's visiting London and finds British history fascinating. But every time he travels to England he's aware he is still a visitor, and when he comes back to New Zealand he know he is coming home.

"Being away from my wife Ronise and my daughter makes me homesick. They don't travel with me, and I wouldn't wish that life on anybody. I'm not complaining but you really have to numb yourself to living on a bus and in hotels. It's not that exciting – that's not why I do it at all. I do it because I get a real kick out of performing and travelling. Occasionally if I've got a couple of weeks in one place we've organised to have them over, but it's not very often. Usually I'm working pretty hard and the times when I've got time off are when I'm the most homesick. Travelling with the band was much easier when I was younger. I've been with the same girl since I was 21 and I'm 36 now. When you're 21 and you're just seeing the world for the first time, that is so exciting. You are a selfish little bastard and you don't care. But as I've got older and spend more time away from New Zealand, the pain of being separated from my family becomes greater. So now if I'm away from home I'd better be working, and if I'm back here I'm in the studio writing and recording or touring. That's my job, I'm still very much in love with my job performing music, and I still find it very challenging and rewarding."

Jon explains he never intends to write a New Zealand song but there are times when he's read through his lyrics and he's realised there is no way anybody from another country could have written that song. "We get to see the world as we tour. It gives an interesting perspective, and it just happens to come out in my music because it's the only perspective I have. It's definitely not a conscious thing. That's just who I am. Lyric writing to me is extremely personal, painful at times and it's hard to do, but it is very satisfying when you get it right. That doesn't happen every time but when it does I think I've managed to deliver what I'm thinking."

Moving on to one of the major events in the career of the band, he talks about that infamous name change brought about because of 9/11 while they were working in LA. "It's pretty silly. When we were just 16 and we were all little virgin heavy metallers, I think we watched the movie *Dune*, a movie based on the Frank Herbert novel, and we thought it was pretty cool at the time. There was a battle at the end called The Shihad, and we thought that was great. We were going to be making a big loud noise so that was perfect – not realising that Frank Herbert had got it from the Arabic Jihad. But I didn't have a clue, I think we mis-spelled it. Obviously later on, in my mid-20s, I thought, 'Oh God, I've got a band called the Holy War!' But by then it was too late. The name had taken on its own meaning.

"For the first time in our career we had a booking agent, a massive management company and a big record deal. It was what we had been fighting for. First I wasn't concerned about our name. I just wanted to get out of there and go home." They stuck it out but pretty soon it became apparent how hard 9/11 had hit America, and suddenly they had the radio department of the record company saying there was no way people would play a band called Shihad on the radio. "They said you've got to think about this. You have to change your name." My initial reaction was no way, but after six months of living in LA and watching the flags come out on every vehicle it started to become an issue. I'd be out doing my grocery shopping and I'd have a chat with someone, and my band would come into the conversation, and once I told them the name that was the end of it!"

After a while Jon was finding he wasn't telling people so that he wouldn't freak them out. "If we had been in New Zealand while that had all been going on I don't think we would have changed our name, but in LA, and seeing it first hand, it was different. We had worked too hard to get this far. It was a dream we'd had ever since we had been at school to have both an American record deal and tour. So there were two options.

Jon Toogood performing with Shihad

If we didn't change our name we could have had that door close on us, or, if we did, we were risking alienating our fans we had built up over 16 years. I think our Kiwi fans understood as much as we did – it felt awful, but they could see why.

"But I never ever felt comfortable being in a band called Pacifier. I went through different phases of 'I'm not going through this again – we are not changing our name back – it is just too hard – we are going to have to wear this like a scar – just like Harry Potter!'" he says, laughing. "We had no choice. It would have to be something we would make cool. Even after two years, when we were touring in Australia, the chant was 'Shihad'. I remember after a show in Perth the crowd had been chanting for an encore, and I turned to the guys and just said, 'Stuff it – let's just change our name back.' And everybody was, 'Yeah, let's do it.'

"We haven't been back to America since then. If people in America like our music enough, then sure we'll go and tour. If they don't, it's no skin off our nose. Especially while George Bush is in power I don't care if I don't see the place. We've recorded an album in Vancouver but people are far more like-minded there. The Canadians have also got that very British thing going on, and they can have a good laugh at themselves, which is something I love about New Zealand and, to some extent, Australia. It's very healthy to take the piss out of ourselves and I think America would be a better place if they learnt how to do it."

The subject of the New Zealand flag comes up. "I've got to admit, it's stupid, but I do feel patriotic when I see our flag. It's a symbol of my country for me. I'm quite proud of it, but if someone comes up with an alternative flag that looks cool, I'd be with it. I realise it's got a union jack and it's similar to Australia, but I think it is quite cool with the red stars."

Jon Toogood is very proud New Zealand has a female prime minister. The fact that she is also the arts minister is an added attraction. "I'm an artist so I have my personal perspective. I think she is a really strong leader, and when I'm away from home I can go, 'Yeah, well, Helen Clark is our prime minister and she told Bush to piss off over the war, and rightly so.' He goes on reflectively. "I'm not happy about the rise of the Destiny Church. I think they are dangerous and narrow-minded, and as we see every time with these modern Christian movements, they are hiding dodgy things themselves. Then there are the Exclusive Brethren paying money to make sure that Labour and the Greens don't get in – that shouldn't happen here, and I find that disturbing. We've got a little way to go in making sure that everyone gets past this foreshore thing, and it's very hard at present because I find the right-wing movement is trying to win elections by turning everything into black and white when we all know something like that is far more complicated. I think the left has to work out how to combat that. One thing I think is really cool is New Zealand becoming more energy-efficient. I think that is a really smart move."

Jon concludes that if New Zealand keeps itself a little bit separate from the European and American way of thinking, and is careful to maintain its individuality, it's going to be fine. He feels New Zealanders lately appear to be proud without being overly patriotic – and for him that can only be a good thing.

"I remember the first time I travelled over to Europe as an adult, and coming back after seeing London in the winter, and going round to my parents and saying thank you very much for deciding to have your family in New Zealand."

TEMUERA MORRISON 18

TEMUERA MORRISON'S HEART AND SOUL ARE IN NEW ZEALAND. IT'S IMPOSSIBLE for him to leave. When he finally drags himself away from whanau and land he finds his culture keeps him company and quickly guides him home. At home is his culture, a culture he worries is being watered down. "We are now brown white," he declares with frustration. His heritage is a mixture of Maori and Scottish/Irish. The European side can take care of itself; its culture is alive and well over the other side of the world. But the Maori side gets Tem's full attention.

Tem's upbringing was typical Rotorua Maori working-class. His dad worked for the Ministry of Works as a civil engineer as well as an entertainer. "I remember the truck used to come and pick him up with all the boys, and while they went off to work Dad would go out looking for pigs and deer. He didn't spend much time with us because he was working at night as a Dean Martin-style crooner. He used to do those Dean Martin songs, 'Well, I'm prayin' for rainin' in California'. Actually he was better than them!" Tem declares.

"There were eight of us, six girls, and my brother and me. For us boys our job was to mow the lawns, and there were enough girls to do the dishes. The big treat for us was a little cup of roasted peanuts on Friday night. We were also fortunate that our mum came from Hangatiki in the King Country, and every school holidays we would be over there working on the farm with our grandparents. That was a big contrast for us. When we'd go over there they would say, 'Here come the townies.' You

Temuera, back left, with his mother and siblings

know what I mean? My grandmother spoke only Maori. She was Ngati Maniapoto, and my dad was Te Arawa. My parents didn't speak Maori in the home. My dad said, 'Don't worry about all that stuff.' I feel their generation were brain-washed. It was the 'Brill Cream' generation where they were influenced by American music and culture. At the same time most of our people were moving to the city where they were discouraged from speaking Maori at school. They were told it had no relevance for the future. I remember when I was quite young being with Dad out in the country when he stopped in the middle of the road and started talking Maori to some of the Ministry of Works people. Right up until that time I didn't realise he spoke it. It was quite a surprise."

From a very young age Tem and his siblings were sent to learn Kapa Haka, Maori performing arts, from their aunties and uncles. "Our dad arranged for my aunties to do a few poi dances and songs at the Rotorua THC Hotel, and that started the regular hangi and concerts at the hotels in Rotorua. It was one of those aunties, Adelaide Maxwell, and her husband Trevor, who gave me and about 20 other cousins, including my Uncle Howard Morrison's kids, cultural lessons in the weekends. They took time to teach us basics in guitar playing, the haka and action songs. Today at a funeral or any family function, we as a family can get up and do quite a performance. We're very special, we Morrisons."

During the 1970s Tem's family performances came to the notice of Tourism NZ and they were invited to perform at cultural events overseas. "People were pretty responsive to the performances. I remember being at the Te Maori exhibition that went to St Louis in the US. We went to a black church service where they were doing their gospel singing – it was a marvellous exchange. They would get up their soloists, and we would get ours up, and then when it came to the haka they didn't have too much of a response. That was it – they were blown away. What do you do after a few Maoris have done the haka? But you know it was all in a good spirit."

Tem feels blessed he didn't end up as just another Jake Heke, one the

Tem top left in family concert group

169

many he would see around Rotorua at the time he was growing up. With his close-knit family it wasn't likely to happen. "The Jakes of the world have no identity with their Maori side, and I don't think they have enough positivism in their lives or knowledge of their culture. When we were singing our own songs for tourists, this became the trigger to find out more about who I was. It led me to go down to the marae and spend time there. When I left school I worked in places like Maori Affairs, driving old people around, and I think I got into that kind of work because of my early involvement with my culture. Knowing I was Maori and being very proud of it.

"My mum is from the King Country. They don't talk that much over there! You can't get boo out of them – you know what I mean? They are just country folk. You just sit on the farm and the only conversation over there is when you hear a car go past every two hours, and they stand up and go, 'Johnsons yep, Johnsons,' and then sit back down again. That's the level of conversation. They were the last haystackers – everybody else had balers. My grandfather was a gun haystack maker. How everyone pitched in was kind of unique, because all the Pakeha farmers had balers. The thing they lacked was labour, and we Maori had all the labour and no balers. So we went around and helped them bale their hay, and they came over and helped us bale our hay. The food on the farm was just so rich and beautiful. I'll never forget the farm food. I also remember going down to milk the cows at 4.30 in the morning with my grandfather, and sometimes waking up in the morning and hearing the noise in the milking shed and knowing we were late, and then getting on our horses to go get the cows. Funnily enough, as I grew up all those kinds of skills like horse riding are ones I've had to use in my career."

Morrison is clearly not a Maori name. Somewhere in Tem's bloodline there has to be an interloper. "The Morrison name comes from Scotland, the Isle of Lewis. In my dad's family we don't worry about that side. Oh, well, yeah, I do, but it's just not a big thing to me. I just concentrate on the Maori side – it's the side that needs my attention. It was James Montgomery Morrison who came over here way back. He married a Ngapui a few generations ago. My grandmother Kahu on my father's side was a famous singer and she married Temuera and that's where I get

Tem takes a break from shooting *Shortland Street*

my name from. Kahu used to say that her mother married an Irishman who learnt from her to speak fluent Maori, and on her father's side it was the same thing, a Scottish fella who married a native woman and he could also speak Maori. Not one of them you meet today can speak Maori, but they had to back in those days."

Tem did one small film in 1973 when he was 13, *Rangi's Catch*, but it failed to ignite any long-term acting ambitions. He continued to do cultural performing but he says he didn't think of much else except having a good time. When he got bored with Rotorua he headed to Auckland. "I decided to join a course in performing arts, and worked as an extra. I did a few TV series and bit parts in movies, and then in 1988 Geoff Murphy cast me in *Never Say Die* for some silly reason," he says, laughing. "It was good fun with lots of action. And then *Shortland Street* came along. I was a little bit different from a lot of other actors I knew at the time as I wasn't thinking of going overseas. I was still getting all the travelling I needed from the culture tours. I was living a privileged life. We have a saying down here in Rotorua that Piu Piu (flax skirt) will travel. I had my Piu Piu!

"I was also doing radio work at Aotearoa Radio, the first bilingual station. I really enjoyed this work. Maori have a particular dry sense of humour and we had a lot of laughs. It was good to hear the Maori language on radio and in New Zealand music."

Doing *Once Were Warriors* has been a career highlight for Tem. He's instantly recognisable in New Zealand, sometimes for the wrong reasons. "Oh yeah, some people see me as this great big horrible beast of a person. I was out shopping with one of my children and there were some other kids in the shop. One of the little girls said, 'Oh, you're that horrible mean fella!' I said, 'I'm not that mean.' But they're just kids being kids.

"I remember when I was doing the movie I was still playing the role of Dr Ropata on *Shortland Street*, and I ended up juggling my schedule between the two. I had one week where I must have filmed about 52 scenes as the doctor, and in the evenings I was rehearsing for *Warriors*. It was frantic, I wasn't able to have a hair cut for Jake's character until the weekend, and we were rolling with *Warriors* on the Monday. Because of this I felt I wasn't quite ready for the violent scenes.

"I knew Jakes. They were here in Rotorua. I grew up with them, and as a teenager I'd see them hanging out at the pubs. I didn't talk to Alan Duff about Jake much. We had a few meetings. In fact everybody was nervous in case they had cast the wrong guy. I took it on my own shoulders. I remember a couple of times I'd look to either side of me and there's no one there, and I'd think, 'Oh shit, I have to do this from within. Ok, let's go.'

"Fortunately for me I could draw on my haka and all that performance energy that comes with it. It was something I did have. If you look at the word haka, ha is our breath and ka is the fire and it's in there somewhere. We've all got the fire in the veins. It's just a matter of tapping into it. You've got to concentrate and go inside your soul and find the volcano, your ihi, your wehi. So in some ways it wasn't a very nice time for me. There were a few moments there where I used to have a little cry to myself. I didn't like doing some of the nasty stuff. Yeah, it was hard to get angry, especially after lunch," he says, laughing again. "I'd say to Lee Tamahori that I felt like going to sleep.

"When we were filming the big scene in the pub, right towards the end, everybody was having their turn for their close-up. Then it came to my turn, and I was buzzing – you know, there was a little vibe in the air, and the intensity was potent. But right at that moment we ran out of time so they cut. I had to do my close-up in the morning, but by then everybody was cold and dead and half asleep, and you've got to pick up your vibe again. We were all nuts by that final week, anyway. When I finished *Warriors* and went back to working on *Shortland Street* I kept swearing at all the nurses! When you do a role like that it lingers with you. It takes a while for all that stuff to wither away. Sometimes it stays there. While it was a great role I'm still haunted by the Jake image. Now I want a romantic role with Angelina Jolie but no one's calling!"

Since *Warriors* a lot of film work has centred on working in America. He says he's never considered living there – his heart wouldn't be in it. "It's too much travelling, too many malls – after two weeks I'm over it. I can go to dinner and talk the talk and walk the walk, bullshit like crazy like the rest of them, pretend I know everybody, and then come home

Tem, right, and an extra, on the set of *The Piano* where he worked as a co-ordinator

again. But yeah, if I got a good film I'd stay, that makes a big difference. But it's still a lot of competition.

"I think Rena Owen is doing it the right way, although she comes home a lot. You've actually got to be there most of the time. I've been tending to go in and out, and at the end of the day your agent needs consistency from you. Down here we are a little bit isolated, which means I've got to work twice as hard when I do get to LA. I've always been the kind of person who goes, 'Well, hey, if things happen they happen.' I believe sometimes it's already written. Some of us have a lucky star above our head and some of us don't. Down here I've got children. I got to feed them and get them off to school."

For Tem it's always good to come home, no matter how many times he's travelled. For him there's nothing like the plane touching that tarmac at Auckland airport. "I go, 'Ahhh,' I breathe a mighty sigh of relief. Just the other day I took the kids over to Maketu on the East Coast and had a great day. It's just the simple life. Go to the beach, get some pipis and fish and chips. I'd just got back from LA two weeks ago and I'd got an invitation to go to Jamaica for some promotional thing. At the same time I was invited to a ceremony at the marae. There was no choice. I ended up in the kitchen carrying the food out. We had a thousand people to feed. I was doing what I used to do when I was a kid before I became famous. I really enjoyed that. I was home. When you're on the treadmill and the heart comes knocking at the consciousness, and says 'Hey! It's time to get off!' it comes back to your spirit and your connection to the land, your turangawaewae."

Tem thinks New Zealanders at times can be "small thinking" while taking the country for granted. He acknowledges he's seeing it all from the point of view of someone who travels a lot, and is always grateful to be back home, but the worrying crime rate hasn't bypassed him. "We're getting a lot of crime from P – methamphetamine – and I think it's getting out of hand. Some of the old values have gone. In our day, if some clown snatched a bag from some old person, they would have been belittled by the community. The matter of respect for our old people is something that is very concerning at present. They've paid their taxes, they need more taking care of, and we need to respect them, not rob them.

"I think Maori have got a long way to go – we need to be driving our language ourselves. We have Maori language week one week a year, and on mainstream TV we get to watch the Maori news 10 minutes a day – it's really patronising and stupid. How long have we been here? In the old days when the Scotsmen and the Irish came here, they all learnt Maori themselves. Now there's still Maori-bashing going on. Sometimes it has made me ashamed of the media. We should be driving the language and culture home because this is what makes us New Zealanders. We fought our battles, and we came from a violent 18th century background. There were tough Irishmen and Scotsmen all coming down here to fight Maori – now some of us Maori have names like Morrison, McDonald and McGregor. We are the living result of those battles. But I think sometimes we Maori are strangers in our own country."

Tem as Jake the Muss in *Once Were Warriors*

The subject of mana comes up. Tem explains part of his mana is his genealogy, which he can trace back to Tama Te Kapua, the captain of a canoe that left Tahiti in 1350, and whose ancestral house still exists in Rotorua. "On that canoe there were 100 people. We and the Tainui people are related from that voyage. They left Tahiti because of land disputes, and overcrowding, so they made the decision to leave. Kupe and a few other people had been down here already and told us of this vast land that hadn't been populated yet. A lot of New Zealanders don't realise that we were quite tribal before we even came here. When all the canoes got here, they were having disputes over who got here first!

"Maori are so mixed blood now. Our genetic mana is diminishing through every new generation. But that's only part of it for me. Mana is also from your deeds in life, because when you do something good you stand out in life, and that becomes something significant, it gives you mana. The recent Maori queen's tangi, for example – well, that's the epitome of mana right there. She worked for it and lived it! And thousands turned up. When you're overseas it's more potent because you miss the land, your whakapapa, your culture and the things that can give you confidence to stand out in the world. What makes me unique is my Maoriness."

Tem's love for his New Zealand is precious, and he sees others eyeing up this hard-fought for land. He sums it up thus, "I'd rather not tell too many people now about New Zealand. The world is small enough as it is. It used to be, 'Yeah, let's promote. Let's wave the flag,' but the more I've travelled the more I think no – let's shut up about it, let's put the toll gate up now. Tell them Australia is a great place to live."

PHIL KEOGHAN

CHECK OUT ANY WEBSITE ON PHIL KEOGHAN AND YOU'LL FIND COUNTLESS PUNCHY descriptions of someone who takes on the world of adventure – and wins. This man runs on super-adrenalin, enough to leave anyone in his wake. His success in the world of adventure television is phenomenal.

Getting him to take time out to talk about being a New Zealander is remarkably easy. His Kiwi identity is in the forefront of almost everything he does, and the suggestion of transferring that bond to another country is immediately dismissed. "You can become a citizen for the sake of wanting to vote or for some other kind of convenience, but I don't think you can take the New Zealander out of somebody no matter what you do. I am still a New Zealand citizen and there is nothing better than travelling on a New Zealand passport. I'll always be a New Zealander."

Phil's family came from working-class England and Ireland. They were coal miners and carpenters. His paternal grandfather was a mechanic, and his other grandfather was a carpenter with his own business on the West Coast. "My political views come from my parents. My dad has a PhD in agronomy – plant science – and my mother is a highly-qualified musician and high school teacher. Their politics came from their professional backgrounds, which involved giving to others. It is also mixed with a worldliness which I've inherited from them. My parents were quite radical in the 1970s. They took off to work overseas with us two kids when I was just three," he says.

The Keoghan family lived in Canada for three and a half years, and the Caribbean for eight. In 1981, when Phil was 13, he was sent back to New Zealand to board at St Andrew's School in Christchurch while his parents stayed on in Antigua. "It was a culture shock for me to go back to New Zealand, even though my parents spoke about it all the time we were away. We didn't have TV, so we would listen to records. Dad would have plenty of books about the country, and they would often play Inia Te Wiata singing Maori songs. So when I arrived in Christchurch to start school, in some ways there was this familiarity – but really everything felt very foreign."

Phil didn't see his parents at all that year. He acknowledges that they made a big sacrifice for him to be flown half way around the world to get a good education. "They didn't feel I was getting a proper education in the Caribbean. We had New Zealand Correspondence School lessons for a while, and they worked for my sister but they didn't work for me. I guess my parents felt I needed more structure to my days. It was probably one of the smartest things they ever did, but it was incredibly tough. For all intents and purposes, I was a West Indian. Although I was New Zealand-born, I had a West Indian accent and mindset. My dad had played representative rugby in New Zealand. The only thing I knew about the game was from the photos of him in the Lincoln College First Fifteen, and what he'd told me. In the beginning I fought the system. I was trying to hold on to my Caribbean identity. But even over there I felt different at times – being one of the few white kids at my school."

The silver lining in Phil's cloud appeared in the school holidays when he was able to travel to the West Coast to spend time with his grandparents. His grandfather was a gunsmith with a proud country-wide reputation. Phil made the under-25 New Zealand shooting team when he was in the fifth form. "One of my best memories is going to Trentham for the New Zealand Champs with my grandfather. I used to hang out in his workshop with him and there are still things that I do today that I learnt from him. He was a real Burt Monro character – he could fix anything. People would send rifles from all over New Zealand to work on because he was so good. I would stand for hours watching him work and I loved doing small jobs for him."

As a young man Phil longed to explore the world. "Travelling with my parents had given me the bug. We are such a small country. We read about all these places and study their histories in school, and we are teased by everything that the world has to offer us. I think that's why New Zealanders have this desire to travel. The bigger countries – such as the US – don't tend to look out much because they're bigger and they see themselves as the centre of the world."

At 23, Phil and his wife Louise, who was then his girlfriend, headed overseas. Both left good jobs in television behind them. "I had worked at TVNZ since I was 18, and then helped to launch TV3. I left all that behind. I had a hunger to do something else. Everybody said we were crazy. We had a job lined up in Canada, and after that finished, with no other work on offer, we headed to New York. We then developed a show called *The E-Team*, which was an environmental adventure-type show for kids. It got picked up by a distributor, and that allowed us to get visas organised. This took almost a year and cost us about $50,000 US in legal costs and expenses. The exchange rate was working against us, so we really bottomed out financially. On top of that, we used our own money to finance *The E-Team*."

The couple headed home to make some money. After a while Phil was able to afford to return to the US. "Only one of us could afford to come back, and that was me." Apartment-sitting became the only way to survive while looking for work. As luck would have it he landed a part in a L'Oreal commercial. "This thing kept paying and paying. I made more money from that one day of work than I had ever made in an entire year on any New Zealand show. It went on running for about three years, and the money kept coming in, so our options changed. It seemed like every time we ran out of money, a cheque would arrive in the mail and just cover our expenses."

In 1994 Phil began a four-year tenure on a Fox morning TV show, which involved travelling around America and doing live stories. "It was an amazing experience. After that long run I formed a company with two Australian guys I had been working with and we sold a number of series, one of them being *Phil Keoghan's Adventure Crazy*, in which I went around the world doing things from my 'life list' such as diving in

179

the world's longest underwater caves – I got paid doing all the things I wanted to do. That show still plays around the world, and I recently saw it on screen in New Zealand. Unfortunately, I never had a piece of the ownership.

"*The Amazing Race* came along in 2000. I had been short-listed for *Survivor*, and apparently it was between Jeff Probst and me. In the beginning I was very disappointed I didn't get it, but now I can see that *The Amazing Race* was probably more in line with what I wanted to do. It's actually not my own show. It was created by a husband and wife team. When I was short-listed for it I thought, 'Oh my God, please don't let me be the bridesmaid again!' Thankfully they picked me."

Although Phil and his family live in Los Angeles, Phil feels very much in tune with what is going on in New Zealand and what it means to be a New Zealander. "The best way to describe a New Zealander is to talk about their attitude to life. Burt Munro was a perfect example. This resourcefulness that we have comes from living in a young country –

Horse riding in Turkey

whatever is needed to make it work, we can do it. That, to me, is what New Zealand is all about, and I hope we never lose it.

"I think people regard the US as a country of friendly, helpful, smart, and creative people who make things happen. But some of our biggest strengths can become some of our biggest weaknesses, and maybe it's because I have a more global perspective on things now that I can make this observation. We understate things, which I feel can be a strength, because people who blow their own horn can be full of hot air. New Zealanders tend to be silent achievers. They just get on and do it. There is a certain charm in being humble about your ability, but it can also mean that in a competitive environment New Zealanders can be left behind and not be taken seriously. We tend to stick with the old 'she'll be right' attitude, and sometimes that's not good enough. It can charm people because it can mean, 'Yeah, I'll give it a go. Give me a pair of pliers, and I'll put it back together.' It's an endearing side to our culture that I love and I don't want it to be lost, but of course there are times when we need to present ourselves differently. There are so many people in New Zealand who are so good at what they do, and yet they allow others who are not anywhere near as talented to take control. They don't need to be wankers about it, but they need to say, 'Hold on a minute. I can do this.'

"It's important to be flexible, read the market place and have a global perspective. A New Zealand friend of mine was telling me about when he had to go in and pitch for a new job for his company in New York. He said he had to do so in a way that was expected of him by the New York executives. But if he was in Wellington and went in with the same aggressive approach they would think, 'Whoa, this guy's been working overseas too much. He's too full of himself.'"

While Phil's own self-help book, *No Opportunity Wasted*, has done very well in the bestsellers' lists, he says he's a long way off from doing an autobiography. "If I'm lucky enough to live a long, full life and if there are some interesting things to write about, then maybe." But not at this time, he says. It doesn't stop him from reading about other New Zealanders. "I've just finished reading Peter Jackson's book. I've also read books by or about A. J. Hackett and Sir Edmund Hillary. Those

Phil, left, belly dancing in Turkey

guys have the smarts. They have the 'she'll be right – I'll make it work' attitude. They've shown others that they can do better than they can, for less money, while still maintaining the quality of the project. "There are so many of our top people in medicine, science and film. They are world-class and we need to celebrate that. As a nation we need to find a way to do that. The tall poppy syndrome is so ingrained that we're reluctant to oversell ourselves – and yet, I'm contradicting myself because this is what makes us charming!

Here in the US, New Zealanders have a reputation for being hard workers, for sticking it out and for using our initiative, and being low-key with it. Which is a very endearing quality. This is very important. There's nothing worse than a bunch of wankers who spend all their time talking themselves up. New Zealanders just get in and do it.

"I was lucky enough to speak to the Prime Minister at a function here in LA a few years ago, and she said that we really need to stop seeing New Zealanders who go overseas as a brain drain, and more of a brain gain. I think she's right but some New Zealanders see those who leave the country as a personal insult. That's been the attitude for a long time. We have a tendency to disown talented people who travel overseas. The most patriotic New Zealanders I've ever met are those who live overseas – they are the best ambassadors.

"In order to change things, we really need to heed what the Prime Minister said. I recently met an old friend here in LA who is a successful medical specialist, and asked her if she'd consider going back to New Zealand. She said, 'Yeah, if they would invite me, but nobody has mentioned it.' What I'm saying is that sometimes we think that people wouldn't come back, but there are a lot of Kiwis overseas who would love to share the knowledge they have gained with New Zealanders back home."

For Phil, being able to go home and try to do this is exciting. But he understands that you don't need to travel to be successful overseas. "Peter Jackson has done all these extraordinary things, and he does this all from New Zealand. This kind of attitude is what we should aspire to. You know, people in New Zealand have come up with great technological breakthroughs in science, proving that. This is something we can do from New Zealand."

Phil believes that New Zealanders are now given more recognition for their overseas achievements than they were in the past. "Fifteen years ago Sam Neill had starred in *Jurassic Park* and a lot of other films, but you didn't see anything about him. All you'd see was somebody from *Shortland Street* on all the magazine covers. Where was Sam Neill? There might have been a little blurb here and there, but nothing like celebrating this great talent. This wouldn't happen now. I was in a pub on the West Coast recently, and this truck driver comes in. He's got grease all over his hands, looking mean as hell, and he walked up to me and puts his hands out. I thought, 'Oh shit, here we go,' and he says, 'Bloody good on you, mate. I saw you on the telly getting that Emmy award and New Zealand's real proud of ya, mate.' I thought, 'Wow, OK.' Here's a guy from the remote West Coast who is connected with New Zealanders overseas. Technology has really helped us make those connections."

But Phil hates the way we are so wary of celebrating our successes.

Especially when the All Blacks are involved. "I still turn on the radio and hear commentators blasting the All Blacks after they've beaten another team 60 nil, and they're talking about how much better they should have done. How can you possibly imply that they're useless? Where does that come from? Does it make us feel better about ourselves to run them down because it makes them more like us? Is that why we do it?"

Phil and his Australian wife Louise enjoy a friendly rivalry when New Zealand and Australia play each other in sport. "We're always the underdog and there's nothing quite as satisfying as beating Australians at sport. I'd hate to be the bullying big brother who loses out to a small country like New Zealand. It makes them look bad!"

There have been plenty of times over the years when he has felt homesick. Home is never far from his mind. "I even feel homesick when I

Phil, left, and crew on a South American trip

see the word 'New Zealand'," he says. The Keoghan family live in Santa Monica in a house overlooking the Pacific Ocean where Phil has many opportunities to reflect on the connection of the Pacific he can see to the shores of New Zealand. "Watching the Air New Zealand planes going back and forth out of LAX nearby makes me feel homesick, but it also acts as a connection for me. I think, 'Oh the bird just flew over.' I love the airline because it's always been the connector. It's the silver bird that flies home and comes back. Last year, I did 12 flights between LA and New Zealand. It was the biggest year I've had since I've been overseas. As soon as I get on the plane, hear the accent, see a few glasses of sauvignon blanc lined up for me, and wrap up in a wool blanket, I feel like I'm home already. When I get home, the first thing I notice is the smell of the air and how green the countryside is. I feel comfortable. It's like Christmas Day to me. I still feel that intensity. We have a place in the Coromandel which is also on the ocean, so we think of it as coming over on the silver bird to the other side of the ocean. On a very clear day you can see our place in the US from here!" And he laughs.

Phil often gets a hard time about his American-sounding Kiwi accent. "I remember once some guy said to me – again it was in pub – I sound like I'm always drinking but I'm not! He said, 'Oh mate, aren't you a New Zealander any more?' I said, 'What do you mean?' He said, 'That yankee accent – what the hell's that?' I said, 'I didn't know you had to sound a certain way to be a New Zealander!' When I was growing up my accent was constantly changing because of all the travelling I was doing. I had a strong Kiwi accent when living at home, but when I left at 23, it just changed again. It's easily influenced, I guess."

The critically acclaimed show *No Opportunity Wasted,* which Phil and Louise – who is also his business partner – produced for television in the US, was picked up by New Zealand's TV2 in 2006. "This meant that after 15 years of being away from New Zealand we came home to live and work for a few months. Our daughter, Elle, who was born in New York and raised in Los Angeles, went to a public school in Glendowie. She loved it and joined the cross-country team, even developing a bit of a Kiwi twang.

"It was amazing for us as a family to live back home for that period of time — to not be on vacation in New Zealand but to be part of what we left 15 years earlier. We worked with many of the crew we had worked with back then so it was a real feeling of familiarity. It was exciting to come back home with a project that was close to our hearts."

Phil enjoys connecting the US and New Zealand in his working life. He organised the shooting of *The Amazing Race* in New Zealand, and has also brought CBS News down under to feature five New Zealand stories, which went out on the US network every morning. "They did extremely well," he says with some satisfaction. "I've always tried to get production down to New Zealand. I feel it's my duty. I work in TV and I think New Zealand should be shown off – I love sharing it with people. I get an immense satisfaction from knowing I have the opportunity to do something like that."

GAVIN SCOTT

GAVIN SCOTT HAS HAD A PROLIFIC CAREER IN BROADCASTING, WRITING AND FILM. His relationship with New Zealand was conditioned by arriving as an immigrant from England at the age of 10 after a six-week ocean voyage. For a boy from a fairly grim northern industrial British city, it was a trip like "going to heaven but without having to listen to the choirs".

His first memories are of seeing the green hills of Wellington from the deck of the *Rangitata*, "sprinkled with houses like hundreds and thousands". His first night was spent in the People's Palace in Cuba Street, where there was a bookshop across the street with an edition of *Sherlock Holmes* he was determined, one day, to own (and did). He also remembers getting out of the train beside the flowerbeds around the art deco clocktower in Hastings, to which his family went, almost by pure chance, into a world of bright sunlight he had never known in his native England. "I thought 'This is all right,'" he says.

"Going to New Zealand at that age was a real-life *Boy's Own Adventure* for me. And in some ways my feeling about the country has never changed. For me it has a magical quality, a sense of infinite possibilities like nowhere else on earth."

Throughout his subsequent travelling and his work in the UK and US, Gavin has kept in close contact with home. His wife is a fellow Kiwi, and their three daughters born abroad are all New Zealand citizens. He relishes every return trip he can squeeze into his impossibly busy schedule. "I love arriving back in Auckland and seeing the red corrugated iron roofs, the quarter-acre sections and the wrap-around verandas. Then there's that wonderful feeling of relaxation where the pressures of the world seem to fade away."

When Gavin began going to school in Havelock North there was the usual teasing at school about being a Pom. "My younger brother Glenn and my sister Fiona very wisely adopted New Zealand accents. But as I was constitutionally bolshy, I refused to, which got me into plenty of playground fights. I took elocution lessons and the Yorkshire accent gradually disappeared and became a more standard English accent, equally 'foreign' but I didn't care by then. My father, Duncan, was Scottish and had a strong Dumfries accent, but he fitted in well wherever he was. My mother, Doris, left school at 13 in England but in New Zealand managed to get on a teacher training course and ended up as principal of a small primary school. She re-defined herself. I think being an English kid arriving in the antipodes in those days definitely made me think about

Gavin Scott (far right) and family on their last day in Hull,
with mother Dori, Glenn and Fiona

my identity, in effect to define myself as I probably never would have had I stayed in England. Incidentally the kids in Havelock misread my signature as Gus, the character in the comic *Me and Gus* stories, and it's been my nickname ever since."

A great opportunity that came out of Hawke's Bay at that time was the beginning of his radio broadcasting career. He began acting in radio plays recorded at 2ZB in Napier and even writing short stories that were broadcast in the children's hour. "We used to record on a Sunday evening and I still remember the excitement of going from Hastings to Napier on the bus with those yellow gestetna-ed scripts in my hand. One of the other kids who acted in those plays was Gaylene Preston, who much later found fame as a film director. There was great theatre in Hastings at that time, too, such as the Group Theatre where I performed with Paul Holmes who was later in classes with me at Karamu High School. I loved Havelock North Primary because it was in an old wooden schoolhouse with a bell and there was a great old teacher called Doug who used to play the violin to us when he got bored with teaching, and I'd sit at the back of the class and read old bound volumes of *Punch* from the 19th century. I got my first love of history from reading the terrific political cartoons they published.

"I wasn't so fond of Karamu High School when I went there, and I don't think the staff, generally speaking, were very fond of me because I refused to participate properly in phys ed and maths and other things that bored me. I had good friends like Conrad Pharazyn and Mike Williams and David Butcher and Selwyn June but I was bolshier than ever, and when my mother saw an advertisement in the paper for a competitive scholarship to Wanganui Collegiate she jumped at the chance to get me out of trouble, and put me up for it. I remember being interviewed by the very erudite headmaster, Tom Urquhart, and telling him my ideas about God being a presence in living things rather than a discreet being and his saying 'God forbid!' but it didn't stop him giving me a chance and off I went, leaving home for the first time at 14 for this very posh school.

"It was quite a shock to the system – cold showers and long morning runs and bullying and fagging and beatings and an endless intricate network of rules – but as far as I was concerned it was all worth it because

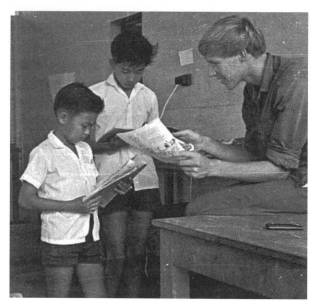

Gavin teaching in Limbang school, Sarawak, Borneo

I got a great education there. Tom Urquhart himself taught English and I suddenly began to understand how you could draw meaning out of texts – like Shakespeare – and go off on a total intellectual riff on a couple of lines, in the course of which you could develop your own philosophy of life. There was a great history teacher called Ken Shadbolt who puffed away at his pipe and made the 17th century and Georgian England and the French Revolution come to life. And on Sunday evenings a group of us would go to the chaplain's house and his wife would feed us Welsh rarebit and we'd watch *The Great War* and other programmes like *Culloden*. Totally mind-expanding."

It was because a former head boy came back to Collegiate to give a talk about his year doing Voluntary Service Abroad that Gavin applied for it too. He did a three-week training course and at the age of 17 found himself teaching English to the children of head hunters (among others) in a jungle school in Sarawak. "I did a lot of reading there too, especially C. P. Snow, and began forming my own philosophy up there in the Murut longhouses and by the banks of the great grey greasy Limbang River. Wrote my first book, too, When I got back next Christmas I wrote this first book – about my experience – while I was earning the money to pay for university by working at the Tomoana Freezing Works. All the old gang from Karamu were doing the same thing, there or at Wattie's cannery. I tried that for a night but the smell of billions of boiled peas nearly drove me off my head."

Growing up in Hawke's Bay had also put him in touch with the physical world in a way life in Hull never had. "We all went picking strawberries and raspberries, thinning apples in the orchards, cutting asparagus. We were out there in the midst of this cornucopia of good things, helping harvest it. There was an intensity and vividness about that which English city life just doesn't bring ... to say nothing of being able to swim in the surf at Ocean Beach and go whitebaiting in the Tukituki River. These were the sorts of things I'd read about it children's books. Now they were happening to me. I think that instilled in me the idea that anything's possible – that life can in fact be quite as interesting as anything in books if you take it the right way!

"And I could go to university, which neither of my parents had – and thanks to a university scholarship it didn't cost any more than I could earn myself. Good old New Zealand! And I'm very glad I worked in the freezing works alongside my dad, too, because, like the years spent working in the fields when we first arrived, it put me in touch with what makes New Zealand tick, how it makes its living in the world. You're not cut off from that, as you are in most industrialised countries. Or at least you weren't then."

Working for both a degree in history and political science at Victoria University and a diploma from New Zealand's first journalism training course, held at Wellington Polytechnic, Gavin married fellow student Jane Cole during 1971, their final year. They were both "terrifyingly young", but full of plans for work and travel. Each then worked for the New Zealand Broadcasting Company "in the days when it was a real public service organisation and the people working for it had the highest standards. Sadly, that's changed dramatically. Now when you turn on New Zealand television you get the impression it's being run by a bunch of money-grubbing hucksters who don't give a damn about the programming, just how many ads they can cram into a given hour. The

NZBC we worked for aimed high and often managed to get there."

In spite of their satisfying jobs the young Scotts left to go overseas, travelling overland across Asia. "The rite of passage in those days was to do one's OE, overseas experience. Every self-respecting young Kiwi headed off into the blue to see what the big wide world was like. We went through places like Kashmir, Afghanistan and Iran that are simply too damn dangerous these days, and the whole world opened up for us."

In London in traditional Kiwi fashion they took on all sorts of odd jobs. Then Jane, who had decided to call herself Nicola, became a film editor in current affairs and Gavin became a journalist, first with *The Times* and then the BBC in radio and TV. Both made documentary films for television, and Gavin began writing novels.

He stood for the House of Commons twice in the 1980s but when it was clear that Thatcherism, which he loathed, wasn't going to be defeated for some time, he dropped both politics and journalism and in 1990 took up a new career as a screenwriter.

"My first gig was when George Lucas's people read a script of mine about Jules Verne and brought me into the team that was writing *The*

Gavin directing *The Battle of Treasure Island*, in New Zealand,
with actor Randy Quaid

Young Indiana Jones Chronicles. Suddenly I was commuting from our home in Richmond, Surrey to Skywalker Ranch in Marin County, California, an amazing experience and a fantastic learning curve. George Lucas was able to recruit great film directors to shoot the TV episodes and Terry Jones of *Monty Python* directed one of my scripts. We became friends and even wrote some scripts together, one of which became a pretty funny animated series called *Blazing Dragons.*

"Then I sold a spec script to Steven Spielberg, which later became the movie *Small Soldiers.* Nicola and I felt I'd done enough commuting and there was a chance of making a career as a screenwriter so we left England and settled near Los Angeles, in Santa Monica. Our three daughters, then 12, 10 and 5, adjusted marvellously well, and our whole family soon settled into the community. Nicola has begun producing feature films and I write both feature films and television series such as *Mists of Avalon, Legends of Earthsea* and more recently *War and Peace.*

"Coming back to New Zealand is very important to me. It's a place in my soul as well as a geographical entity – there's a peace about the country that's rare in the world, a gentleness and kindness about New Zealanders which I treasure. But at the same time it's full of people who know what's going on in the world and have a great perspective on it too.

"I love meeting up with Kiwis overseas. There's the simple pleasure for a start of being able to talk about places you know and have in common. I have to say the New Zealand consuls I've dealt with over the years here in Los Angeles have been really good at bringing together the expatriate community. If there is a visiting New Zealand film-maker or artist, the consul makes sure they get the best possible chance to meet the most helpful people in LA as well as their fellow Kiwis, which is good for both sides."

Gavin agrees it's possible he could have accomplished many of his career achievements if he had stayed on in New Zealand. Continuing working for the NZBC in the 1970s would have given him very much the same work experience as working for the BBC, "but you always want to test yourself in the biggest possible arena. Now I feel equally comfortable, if in different ways, in the UK, the US and NZ. One of the

With all three daughters, Chloe, Laura and Rebecca, and wife Nicola

great things that the improvement in communications over the years has brought about is I can be a film-maker operating out of LA and also work in New Zealand. Our generation is enormously lucky to have the choice. You can have all the benefits of being in New Zealand without feeling cut off from the world, as you were when it took six weeks to get there by boat!"

He muses about what he misses about New Zealand. "Perhaps not a tangible thing but a lost time, that wonderfully innocent country of the early '60s when people of all races seemed to get on so much better. When we arrived in Hastings we lived with Maori families and my father worked alongside Maori in the freezing works as I did in the university holidays. There was an ease between the peoples which doesn't seem to be the same today, and I regret that. And I've already mentioned the broadcasting ..."

Gavin is reluctant to pin down national characteristics that make New Zealanders "different from other people" but suggests Kiwis tend to be too modest, too reluctant to stand out. "In America, you've got to say who you are, what makes you distinctive and interesting, because people expect you to impress them. New Zealanders don't seem comfortable doing that – which in some ways is admirable, and in other ways mean they sometimes undersell themselves."

When it comes to the Kiwi work ethic, however, Gavin has no reservations. "Coming back to New Zealand as a first-time director on *The Battle of Treasure Island* I was completely bowled over by how supportive people were, how hard they worked and that great Kiwi can-do spirit. If you have a creative vision there are people in New Zealand who will go out of their way to help you realise it.

"I think that is one of the reasons New Zealand has been so successful in films. The kind of people who came to New Zealand in the pioneer days, then continued to emigrate, are the kind of people who have probably more initiative that the average. In America if you've got the money to spend you can get anything done. In England it is probably harder to get it done whether you've got the money or not. In New Zealand it will get done and money is not what it's all about."

Having lived in both Britain and the United States, he'd like to see New Zealand take a greater leadership role in the world because he thinks the values New Zealand embodies – tolerance, lack of fanaticism, looking after one another, protecting the environment we live in – are more crucial than ever to the future of the planet. "It's the kind of thinking the world really needs, and I'd like to see New Zealand asserting it. We're a small country, but that doesn't mean people won't listen to us. It's the force of example, it's the 'still, small voice' when the big boys have shouted themselves hoarse. If more of the rest of the earth could be like New Zealand, I think the human race might have a better chance of survival. Let's hope people pick up on that."

His main theme, though, is how glad he is that his parents decided to come out and live in New Zealand. "I think it was the best decision they ever made," he says . "It certainly gave me a life I would never otherwise have had – and I'm eternally grateful for it."

LUCY HOCKINGS

WHEN LUCY HOCKINGS FIRST WORKED FOR THE BBC IN 1999, SHE WAS TOLD to take elocution lessons to rid her of her Kiwi accent. Now she is heard around the world as one of the valued newsreaders on BBC World. "I don't think I had a strong accent to start off with, and it's certainly softened since I've been living here. I'm not a natural mimic and I found the lessons really hard. When I'm reading the news I'm not meant to be playing a part. I'm meant to be myself conveying a message. It has been a huge battle for me, trying to get rid of the vowels." After recent management changes in attitudes, her accent doesn't seem to be a barrier now.

Lucy grew up in Auckland in Mt Eden, a relaxed childhood spent in bare feet and being told by her mother to only "come home when it gets dark". She says she had an incredibly good secondary education.

"I went to Kristen School on the North Shore. That school was one of the great gifts of my childhood. I had wonderful teachers and the classes were small. For them there was no tall poppy syndrome – it was okay to achieve. To have had that in your teenage years is a great thing. I became head girl and a regional debater. My brother Liam was a special needs student who was ahead of me, and he would never have got as far in life if it hadn't been for that school.

"When I left I did a journalism degree. Everyone thought I'd do law so I think it was a lucky escape. I went to TVNZ when I graduated, and worked as a producer of the *Holmes Show* on TV One. Here I was, this little sweet thing of just 21, just out of journalism school, and thrust into the tough Holmes arena. The executive producers were hard on the producers, and it was very much a baptism of fire."

Lucy wanted to travel, and grew up with a map of Paris on her bedroom wall to remind of her where she hoped to be heading. "In 1999 when I turned 22 I thought if I stayed in New Zealand I'd be married at 25. Life was meant to be so much more than that. It was time to leave. Luckily I had a boyfriend who was happy to do some backpacking around Europe with me. Eventually the relationship folded, partly because he wanted to go home – I think he thought I'd follow. As it turned out I didn't. But I didn't ever imagine I'd love travelling so much."

Now living in London with her partner, Canadian director-producer Jason Breckenridge, she says London has been a good compromise for the couple as neither wishes to live in each other's home country.

"When I arrived in London after a year of backpacking I looked up some old TVNZ people who were working here, and did some work at CNN and Reuters. Then the BBC opportunity came up. As a producer I had no aspirations to go on air, but at a very drunken Christmas party one of the bosses asked if I'd like to try it out. I had already done work as a reporter on screen in New Zealand but I had never read auto-cue. After a few practice runs they said yes, and I went on an overnight shift. My first couple of shifts I was absolutely petrified. It was over the Christmas period and I remember they went to the news after the Christmas movie which was *Titanic*. And of course I come on and they've got this massive audience who have decided to watch the headlines before they toddle off to bed, and they all complained. It wasn't huge but it was enough to pull me off air.

"They complained about my accent. 'What's an Australian doing reading the news? Can't you get a nice British girl?' The BBC said I'd have to go away and work on my accent. That's when I had the elocution lessons. I came back and did a few more shifts but it hadn't made much difference so I went back to producing. I thought, well, this is my niche. I'm a good producer and I was promoted to bulletin editing and was doing that as a free-lancer and travelling when I wanted to. I was having a fantastic time in London so I was fine with it.

Lucy Hockings reading the news for the BBC

"When they were desperate they would ask me to read the news, and I started doing it more and more. One day a talent coach told me she had used tapes for her students of me reporting in New Zealand. 'I don't know what they're worried about,' she told me. 'They should put you on International and I'm going to tell the management this. The last thing you should think about is your accent. The moment you forget about it you will become more natural and comfortable on air. No one will notice.' I took her at her word and then the management changed and I was offered my own show. It's never been mentioned again. Ironically my boss who gave me grief was a New Zealander. She'd been at the BBC for twenty years and she had been given grief for her accent, and she was super conscious of it."

Lucy didn't go home very much at first but now with a new baby she'll return home to visit family and friends more often. "I want this child to have a strong Kiwi identity. Jason teases me about that all the time because he doesn't feel Canadian very strongly. He says not a day or a dinner party will go by without my bringing it up. I've already got the Buzzy Bee and the sheepskin and little merino vests. It's still so much a part of who I am. The baby will still say 'jandals' and 'togs' in an English accent! I want it to have the language of New Zealand. I'm going through the rigmarole of getting an English passport at present and I have to swear allegiance to the Queen. It will be a very strange feeling when I don't feel remotely English. I have only Scots in my heritage."

Lucy has a group of New Zealand friends in London who are her touchstone. They understand where she comes from. "I think New Zealand women are very different from English women – for a start they are 20 years ahead of English women. We're very assertive about what we want and we know we deserve it. We won't be messed around. We have different expectations of relationships, whether that's a business relationship or a personal one. We expect equality. It's always 'girls' or 'ladies' here, and trying to be called 'ms' is a struggle.

"I'm proud to be from a place where so many positions of power are held by women. New Zealand women's expectations of men and society are something you don't get anywhere else. I can imagine that a man who's not from New Zealand would find it hard to relate to us – they probably think we're being difficult! When I was younger, in the late '70s and early '80s, there were big campaigns to be a tidy Kiwi, and people were influenced by those messages. The message when I was a young girl was 'Girls Can Do Anything'. Jason says, 'Oh, you had that slogan – girls are better than boys', and I tell him, 'No we didn't!' But the message was imprinted on my generation that we can do anything. It's an interesting one when it's combined with other things I *don't* like about New Zealand such as that self-deprecating, modest don't-push-yourself-forward thing. I've found myself a victim of both those things – yes, I'm a woman and I can do anything, but as a Kiwi it's not worth it."

She thinks that men get ahead in Britain, particularly in organisations like the BBC, because of their confidence – especially if they are upper-class. "As a New Zealander I've laboured under a false impression that if I just worked hard I'd do well. It doesn't happen – it's not enough. You have to be a self-promoter and you have to work the room. It's partly because of that tall poppy thing – it does still exist. And I guess that's still part of who I am as a New Zealander – contrary to my wonderful schooling. You should never puff up your chest and hail your attributes from the rooftops, you should work very hard and you will get recognised. I remember someone at the BBC saying years ago, 'The problem with you antipodeans is you all sound uneducated.' I thought, 'You're right!' While being outraged I also believed it. That tapped into that insecurity we have as a nation. But, you know, I think we are growing out of it now.

"I don't think it helps that we come from a culture where men can't express themselves, where the thing that binds the country together is rugby – it's a violent game. It's about the tough bloke. Men cheer if they see a few fists going on in the scrum. I think a lot of the country's dark side is about a dark male culture. It's a brutal environment, and our ancestors came to a very brutal land and had to get tough very quickly. I don't think it is easy being a young man in New Zealand."

One of the most disturbing things for Lucy about going home is the lack of curiosity that she senses in other New Zealanders. "One of the greatest attributes we have as human beings is curiosity – that's why I'm a journalist. People will ask you only one question about your life in London, or they'll just say nothing." They will then begin to talk to her about what's happening in New Zealand, pointing out how much better things are in New Zealand. "I'm saying, 'Have you been to England?' 'No, but it rains all the time and it's polluted.' And I'll say, 'Yeah, but there's pollution in Auckland, and it takes forever to get to work. The reality is New Zealand has a lot of the same problems.

"Ok, there is so much to be proud of in being a New Zealander. There is a renaissance, there's a strong national identity coming through which is hopeful. But then there is a flipside – it becomes parochial and narrow-minded. The endless stuff about the America's Cup! No one gives a shit in the world. It was barely covered in Switzerland, and they won it! We like to think we are taking on the world – and yes, in a very narrow way we are – but it is made into this enormous thing.

"New Zealanders think they have a monopoly on nature – there are no other beautiful countries in the world. There is only New Zealand. I ask if they have been to Britain. It is really beautiful. We don't have a monopoly on a good quality of life. It is undoubtedly incredibly beautiful – no one disputes that. But where is that insecurity coming from? We need to be aware we are part of a global community and that we have unique things to offer. Let's think more about how we can engage with the rest of the world.

"I'm very scathing about how the news is handled at home – I'm sure there are statistics to prove this, in that there is a decrease in the amount of foreign news and an increase in the amount of news about New Zealanders caught up in something overseas. If it's going to be an international story, you have to find the New Zealand connection. It's not followed up with 'Lets have a look at the bigger picture here.' The introspection is getting worse. The people who believe they are British although living in New Zealand are dying. My grandmother's generation always looked towards England, which meant that they still wanted to hear about the rest of the world. Now it's becoming a more regional base. I think that's appalling, and every time I go home it shocks me. You've got to look outside this tiny country to the rest of the world because you could learn a lot. The only way to survive is to be global player. It's vital for the country and the economy."

On the other hand she admires the emergence of the Maori and Pacifika cultures. "I think the isolation of the country means that people have the freedom to be themselves, and you see that in the music and the clothing and other things. The Pacifica influence in Auckland, that's the upside of the isolation."

The homesickness is there, indeed it comes and goes. "Oh yes, listening to *Fat Freddy's Drop*, if I go into a café or a shop here in London and hear them, I'm like 'Ooohh.' I have this cringe thing, but when I see the 18-year-olds on the tube with their back-packs and their New Zealand flags, I want to take them home and feed them. Or I'm like, ditch the flag and try and have a proper experience, see what it's like to go to another country and absorb it, rather than feeling this need to automatically isolate yourself by waving the New Zealand flag wherever you go. I miss the summer, the light, the cicadas and the sauvignon blanc, the beach and feijoas. There can be moments of intensely wanting that unique experience. It's unique to my childhood, although I'm sure it's common to a lot of people. But I haven't thought about wanting to move home. I think if something traumatic happened it would always be my bolt-hole, it will always be my home not matter how long I'm away. Knowing it's there provides me with a sense of security."

She went past her primary school when she was home last and found you couldn't move for cars as people picked up their kids. "I got the feeling no one lets their kids walk home from school – let alone with bare feet. It's sad that it's part of my Auckland childhood that doesn't exist any more. You know, I think that a lot of my friends moved back home to give their children the childhood they had in the 1970s, and it simply

Lucy on location for BBC in Europe

can't be found any more."

As far as her identity is concerned, Lucy says it's been hard living in the UK which has its own strong sense of identity and history. "I've been thinking about it a lot and trying to pin it down – working in such an English organisation as the BBC and being so public. Everyone at work knows I'm a New Zealander – it is referred to all the time. I can't escape it. There can be a slightly condescending view in that arrogant Brit way towards people from the colonies. And I think that I've had to be better because of it. It's been very important to me to retain my identity. I'm very proud to be a New Zealander – a lot of people who like me on air think I have a lot more warmth than other presenters. I hope it shows in other ways in how I interview people. As a journalist working in different parts of the world, I find I do well by treating everyone as an equal.

"That's partly because of where I'm from and that ability to get on with anyone. I don't think New Zealand is egalitarian. It's not totally a socialist egalitarian. My dad is a farmer and he might own half the North Island, but you don't know that. They have to take you at face value and that's why we can get caught out because we don't know the games we should play in other countries. We don't come from a place that has that same kind of structure. I think we need to work on identity – it has to be more than about the All Blacks.

"When I say I'm a New Zealander, people's eyes light up, I don't think many people have had a bad experience from New Zealanders. And to come from a place that's really special, you get to feel unique. I hope we never lose that."

MICHAEL SERESIN

WHEN CINEMATOGRAPHER MICHAEL SERESIN TALKS OF HIS UPBRINGING HE REVEALS a typical childhood in 1950s' New Zealand, but very much coloured by the influence of his European heritage. "Most people at the end of the day went home and had their tea at five – Dad went out into the garden and Mum did her knitting. My old man would have his friends around for a drink before they went out for dinner and ended up at the theatre. In other words, my parents lived a more cosmopolitan life, and I know which I preferred."

His parents' homes were filled with books and magazines; the *New Statesman* and the *New Yorker* were strewn about while passionate political discussions filled the air. His teens were spent watching foreign films and he became keenly aware of the artistic world outside New Zealand. "It was hypnotic, it was seductive – I fell in love with Italian cinema," he remembers. It is no surprise that at the age of 22 he left home, with a romantic vision in his head, for the sophistications of Rome.

In 1992 Michael established the Seresin Estate winery in the Marlborough Sounds where he enjoys show–casing chefs from around the world – plus a few of New Zealand's own.

Speaking from his home in London, (he has a second home in Italy), in his articulate and sometimes gruff manner, it is clear he still bears the same frustrations with his homeland as he felt in his younger years. "I find it the most negative nation in the world," he despairs. "You might say to someone, 'It's a beautiful day, and the answer will come back,

'Yeah, but it's going to rain tomorrow.' You know what I mean? When the state of the Middle East is discussed people will comment to me that it must be great to be in New Zealand when you are back there. And I say it is brilliant because you feel very safe and detached from everything. But also for me there is a negative side to that – New Zealanders are not very interested in the rest of the world. We're not a curious nation."

He has no idea why this is so. "I go to our little village in Italy and my greengrocer will be informed enough to talk to me for half an hour about a movie I've done, and I'll also find that with some of my more interesting friends in Wellington. But in the rural areas they don't give a toss. 'Nice day, isn't it?' and that's it."

Michael's father was Russian and his mother English. He believes it's of no concern where you're born; what matters is where your folks come from. "That's where your roots often are, genetically, spiritually or emotionally, even if you're not aware of it. My mum said to me 10 years ago, 'I knew from when you were five or six that you would get out of New Zealand as soon as you could.' I said, 'What do you mean?' She never really explained, but she was right, because when I was 22

Michael with his parents Rachael and Harry

I bought a one–way ticket out of there. Mother herself was brought out to New Zealand when she was about two. She told me her own mother hated it, and they had two or three goes at going back. Mother loved New Zealand, but she used to visit us in London a lot and was always saying she'd love to live here in a little cottage in Oxfordshire, so I guess genetically my predisposition is towards the old world."

Through frequent visits to Wellington over the years Michael has a keen sense of the changes his home town has gone through. "Look at Wellington which physically is a very beautiful city – there's a sort of aggressive quality about it. They've built these buildings out of black glass and they've turned what was a small town into a city that's trying to be a mini–LA without the architecture. There are great things in New Zealand like the landscape, which we Kiwis are pretty good at stuffing up. We don't seem to be good at respecting it in terms of what we build. Using housing construction as an example, a bloke could build a bach out of an old car case, and it sort of fits in with the landscape. But now we build these places that are on the tops of hills, and we flatten land and put a house on it and it sits there without any respect for nature. I've become more sensitive to it down south where I see it happening a lot.

"The fact that we have GM – genetically modified foods – down there is just idiocy. We should have been the organic garden of the world, two little islands stuck in the middle of the ocean, and what do we do? Some onion farmer says, 'I can't flog my onions to ... wherever,' and we get GM. The country is going to be polluted with it. I'm not saying I'm against it in principle, but we need to know more about it. I was talking to a Maori bloke recently about it and he told me his granddad has always had an organic garden. Why doesn't everyone do that?"

In June 2006 Michael Seresin was invited to participate in a powhiri organised by the New Zealand Drama School in Wellington. "It was probably one of the most moving things that's ever happened to me there. I've a very strong and positive feeling about the future of the country if these kids are representative of it. They were speaking Maori and they told me it is part of their schooling, and I think that's brilliant because if anybody has got any soul in New Zealand it's Maori, not us whiteys. Their whole culture has disappeared and they are living off booze and

God knows what else. And there seems to be a terrible lot of violence among Maori kids as a result of this."

He goes on to say that overall he doesn't feel a very strong New Zealand identity. "I'm not interested in sports, for instance, but I love it when they do a good film." Mention of the infamous tall poppy syndrome brings a quick response. "It's so negative. Believe me, I find New Zealand the most negative nation in the world. It permeates life there, and I don't think people are aware of it. We're not a joyful nation, whether it's the Anglo Saxon heritage or whatever, I don't know. By and large, living in New Zealand is really easy and that may not be a good thing. Recently I was in Lodz in Poland and I walked around the Jewish museum and felt a real sense of history. It doesn't alter one's life, but I think by osmosis it does.

"For example, I find the architecture in most New Zealand towns fucked. I remember Wellington when I was kid. Manners Street used to be quite beautiful and colonial, but it's filled with ugly, cheap and nasty buildings now. I think these kinds of things change people. It doesn't make you better or worse, it just makes you different. There are more than four million people who live there now. They must enjoy it. Some might not have a choice. They can't all be masochists."

There's also frustration with the Kiwi's dismissive attitude to any criticism. "If you say anything critical, they say, 'If you don't like it here you can just fuck off,' and that's as far as the discussion goes."

He adds, "I love the old world way of doing things. Our pioneering spirit, for example, means we have a go at anything, and I love that. On the down side we know everything immediately." He goes on to quote an Italian who on occasion comes out to the vineyard from Italy to make the Seresin Estate olive oil. "People here – they only stick at jobs for five minutes. How does anybody find out anything?" he says. Michael's answer to him is it can be put down to the 'she'll be right' attitude. "There is a reluctance to be seen to be passionate about anything. Which I guess is open to all sorts of interpretation from 'Its fine, it's all done' to 'It'll do for the time being.'"

Michael's father enjoyed an active Wellington social life in the 1950s–'60s, based around home and entertaining, the Chamber Music Society and concerts. Most of his friends were knowledgeable regarding world events and Michael was brought up hearing politics discussed regularly. "I remember in my teens the arguments over personal liberty, the Korean War and Vietnam and much more. I would wonder how those people knew these things. It was a huge awareness for me, but these people were a minority. I don't recall having similar discussions with my contemporaries."

Michael's parents split when he was just four; his mother took him along with his sister to live with her family in New Plymouth. "We had a rough old time there, Mother was an extremely beautiful woman, the sixth and last child by a few years in a big Victorian working–class family. She took us back to the family with her tail between her legs. She had married this dashing Russian and it hadn't worked out, and boy did they make her suffer. We weren't very aware of it when we were kids but there was that sanctimonious judgemental quality of Kiwis which is still pretty strong today. You know, you see it in the letters to the paper and in a lot of the opinion pieces. There is a sort of joylessness to it. When I was 12 Mother met another bloke and got married again and we moved over to Tauranga. I think that's when things settled down.

"I had a good upbringing. My mother worked very hard and she was a responsible person. But I always remember there was that element of wealthy members of the family treating us like shit. I remember as a kid running up

Michael on the set of *Angela's Ashes*

to the front door and being told by some stern aunt to go around to the back door. My mother was head–strong and free–spirited, and they made her suffer for it."

When Michael turned 15 his mother sent him to his father in Wellington where he was promptly enrolled as a boarder at Wellington College. "It was okay for me, it made me very independent. By the time I was 17 I had moved into a flat opposite Victoria University where I had classes in philosophy, political science and history. I was there for only two years. I wasn't cut out for study." Along with a miniscule film industry there was one salvation for a culture–hungry youth and that was the university's film society where Michael saw as many films as he could. There was also John O'Shea who ran Pacific Films, and was a friend of Michael's father. "He was a lovely man, more of a father to me than my old man was. He treated you like an equal. Working with him instilled in me the rigours of film–making albeit in a very pioneering style in the 1960s."

His youth spent watching movies further introduced him to a European cosmopolitan life, and in 1965 he felt ready to take the biggest gamble of his life and move away from Kiwi isolation. "I think I was incredibly immature. I was already married to Deidre with a daughter, Leah, and all I had was £250. I went to Italy by myself and lived on £7–8 a week. I had left my young family in Wellington and it was a few months before they could join me. I didn't know what I was doing, really. I wasn't thinking of the consequences. I spent a brilliant year in Rome but did very little in film. That didn't happen until I came to London in 1967. I didn't know anybody in Italy, I didn't speak Italian, and I spent my time walking around the streets. I lived in a tiny little room in a pension and I discovered Italian life, which I love. Rome is perhaps my favourite city in Europe. Now I have a home in Italy which I've had for 25 years."

Within a couple of years of leaving home a very determined Michael had his first job on a movie. "I've only just thought of this now but it probably comes from not coming out of a traditional class system, say like in England, that I had such confidence." Now with a fulfilling life on the other side of the world, interspersed with occasional return trips to New Zealand, Michael finds little time for undue sentiment towards his home country. "I never feel homesick, absolutely not." But he concedes,

"I was in Europe somewhere recently and there was the smell of the sea and I admit there was a little bit of nostalgia for me."

The impressive kitchen designed for him by Peter Gordon in the old boatshed by the vineyard, which is used on occasion as a restaurant, is 50 feet from the sea. There he has the pick of pipis and cockles for some of the popular dishes cooked for his friends and visitors, served alongside wines produced in the Seresin vineyard. His appreciation of good wines was synonymous with his home life in the early 1960s as a young man in Wellington. "Wine was virtually absent in New Zealand then. Because of the prohibition approach to alcohol, there was an almost religious intolerance of people laughing and having a good time. People would drink to get drunk but for my old man it was part of enjoying a good meal. We always had a good wine on the table for friends. When I went to live in Rome you could walk into a bar at 8am and have a wine and eat a pastry and sit at a table and read the paper. It was a revelation for me."

Over the years spent in Italy Michael became friendly with Italian wine–growing families and considered buying a vineyard himself but he lacked the confidence to do business in Italy. "A friend of mine introduced

Michael on the set of Harry Potter and *The Prisoner of Azkab*

me to Cloudy Bay wines when I was on a trip to New Zealand, and I went to visit Marlborough and I liked it. Because it was close to Wellington I seriously began to consider a vineyard. I think there was probably in a subconscious way, a return to my shallow roots – maybe by osmosis my dad trying to bring culture to Wellington. It was synonymous with a civilised life. There is something civilised about making wine. I know that sounds pretentious and middle–class, but I can't think of any other way of saying it. Being a long–term thing, maybe in a way it's the antithesis of life in New Zealand. On a positive note, I'm sure I've achieved a lot of things in Marlborough that would have been difficult to achieve elsewhere, and that is a heartfelt comment."

While he admits he doesn't follow New Zealand politics closely, Michael is sometimes reminded of the results. "Recently when I was in the South Island I picked up a pair of slack–jawed teenagers, hitching, 'Nice car, you're lucky,' they said. I told them I'd worked hard for it; luck has nothing to do with it. When I asked them where they were heading they told me they were on their way to WINZ – Work and Income New Zealand – in Blenheim. I'd had to ask them to explain what WINZ was. 'Are you English?' they asked. I corrected them. 'You don't sound it!' These kids were unemployed and they were going to get money from the government, and they were only 15. 'Why aren't you at school?' 'I got kicked out because of smoking dope,' one of them said with a smirk. I told him that was really smart. He just threw his shoulders back with an ever bigger smirk. 'Actually that's about the dumbest thing I've ever heard. Doing something like that at school is really stupid.' The other kid interrupted and started going on about how they couldn't get any work. 'The notion that I work my arse off and the money that I give to the government goes to you guys sticks in my throat. You're healthy, fit young men and here it is 10.30 in the morning and you're going off to collect your money. I own a vineyard and we employ kids like you all the time. Heaven help us if you're the future of this country. We should pull the plug and let it sink back into the Pacific.'

"At the vineyard we employ 40–50 seasonal workers, and where do they all come from? Fiji. Very few are local. These two kids could have done that job with their eyes closed. I think every country has an element

Michael Seresin

of that, but I just find it more pervasive in New Zealand. I think that life there is so easy, and maybe that's part of the problem."

Spending most of his time overseas has meant he hasn't kept a close watch on New Zealand's bourgeoning film industry. On occasion he has worked in the country doing commercials. "The New Zealand crews are really good. They're making some good stuff out there. It's a huge industry. It's proportionate to the size of the country, thanks to Peter Jackson."

Lauding New Zealand's 'pioneering spirit', he acknowledges there have been many successes. In some areas, the country has some way to go, he feels. "The food revolution is not as great as some people think.

There is still a lot of crap around. Some people open a café and serve coffee but they may have sweet floury scones, the kind I would have got from the milk bar or dairy back when I was a kid. But sure, the quality of food overall has improved." Warming to the subject he continues, "But New Zealand exists on slogans which I feel uneasy about. There used to be that Air New Zealand slogan, 'Pride of the Pacific', and I hate those words 'pride' and 'proud'. Every province has a slogan, the country's got a slogan, and companies have their slogans. I don't feel comfortable about it. It's a form of inferiority complex or whatever. It's probably just part of being a youthful nation.

"I have a friend who has lived overseas and recently returned to Wellington, and she has found that her friends don't want to talk about where she has been. They are just not interested. They are threatened by it, or whatever. She's gone back there with a lot of experience and she did more in a month here in London than I do in a year – going to art shows and to the theatre and so on. But she says now back in Wellington she doesn't want to just talk about the weather – there are so many other things to talk about.

"Just the notion that when I go back there that I can't talk about what I'm doing because New Zealanders aren't interested or curious – I don't understand it. I don't know where it comes from. It's frustrating. Somebody said to me the other day, 'You know New Zealand has got the best coffee in the world.' I said, 'Bullshit!' They said, 'Oh, you can't get a decent cup of coffee in America.' I said, 'I don't even want to have this discussion with you. It's knowledge based on ignorance.'"

DAVE DOBBYN

ALTHOUGH DAVE DOBBYN HAS TRAVELLED THE WORLD MANY TIMES, HE IS very much a home boy. This deeply religious man's confidence in a re-emergence of a stronger, more community-minded New Zealand knows no bounds. "Yeah, I think it's in our nature to really screw it up, but in my belief system there is always another question to ask. I refuse to get cynical and bitter. I spent a lot of years doing that and you can let that run away with you. I still hold out hope that New Zealand is the perfect place to construct a multi–national community that can live in peace and stay unarmed. And we can export that peace to somewhere else."

The solution for him personally is in his song-writing, and he will continue to write. His conversation is an entertainment all of its own, full of laughter at the end of every second sentence. Then he deftly changes tack. But his message is consistent – from his heart.

"We lived in a Joseph Savage-Labour nirvana of state housing in Glenn Innes in Auckland. I was brought up as an Irish Catholic. It was a full on, extremely bureaucratic way of life. Bodily functions were regulated back then, let alone fiscal policy! I was part of a family of five kids and we all earned our own independence from one another. Dad was a bus driver and caretaker, and we were kind of meat and potatoes people, working-class they call it. My mother is fifth generation, and my father second generation of Irish descent, which has allowed me to hold an Irish passport. It's very handy because I find if I travel on my New Zealand passport in America I'm suspected of being a spy or whatever.

There's a gremlin in their machine that labels me a shoe bomber. They can be ferocious and very paranoid over there. I think it's the red curly hair," he says, laughing.

Dave went to Sacred Heart College in Glenn Innes, where his father worked as a caretaker for 20 years. He describes his school days in uncompromising terms. "A real culture of violence with lots of caning. We spotty little nerds at the back of the pack on athletic days were much marginalised by the fitter prefects. We didn't bother competing, and for that reason we were relegated to being bums. In some ways we were the intelligentsia, the élite. It was kind of good. I felt like a handicapped person or a fat person. I could relate totally to people who were on the outer. I was very short, so it was like being in a kind of freak show.

"I learnt to entertain people, and to get out of trouble, which is incredibly important when you are being attacked – attacked with all guns blazing and the horror of the Catholic hierarchy raining down on you, and the wrath of the Lord himself. It was a state of constant panic at all times, anxious as hell. I lived in my dreams and the music I heard. I'd sit by the radio from a very early age. We had a radiogram and a record player, and I'd sit at night and just turn the dial and get into the world of radio. I'd play Beatles records over and over again, anything my father had, Louis Armstrong and Bing Crosby and bad Irish music along with the good stuff. I was like a sponge. Anyway, that's the way I remember it. It was probably a lot more mundane than that. Everything was so intense then. It took me a few years to recover from being young."

Not long after he started his musical career Dave took off to Sydney to work and live, and he stayed there 10 years before returning to New Zealand. "I definitely felt I'd be restricted in my career if I stayed in New Zealand. But I'm pretty comfortable anywhere as long as my whanau isn't too far away. I can prove it. A couple of years ago I was in the middle of the Saharan desert on a camel, and I got a text from my daughter back home, so yeah, the front yard is getting bigger all right.

"It's nice to think that New Zealand has the greenest politics and the whole deal, but I fear the reality can be something else. Every time I fly back from somewhere like America, I'm 12 hours flying over nothing, and I'm coming into my home town, and I look down and there's a traffic jam. I've travelled all that way, and there is exactly the same problem at home. On the deeper level I feel there is a way people here can co–exist and foster the life we are all dreaming of for our kids. I think people elsewhere find our socialism quite exotic. It's from the Maori and the Pacific Island cultures, the combination of all that, and for us of British and Irish descent it offers the opportunity here to maybe get it right."

Dave says he was watching some old footage of Bastion Point when Maori were walking across to grieve but weren't allowed to by the police. Seeing that blue line sent a shudder through him. "You know, that's only in our recent history. There are concepts of the heart that people understand now – you can feel them through the Maori language and through its richness. There is a communal heart that is precious to Maori culture and we are unaware of how much we absorb it. I think it comes from when you've got mentors who are happy to serve the community

Dave playing in th'Dudes

and fill it with grace and wisdom. Many of the Maori stories are very poetic in their telling of how we got here and who we are.

"One of the great things about being in New Zealand is the weather. I love the way it changes all the time, and the light is never the same. So many of us live near the water and I think there is something deeply grounding about that. We have some American relatives who recently spent three weeks of the summer up north with us in our bach. It's a great spot, you're on the beach, you're alone, and you're just enjoying one of the simple things of life, looking for shells and swimming. The American kids didn't have any idea what that meant – to just talk about nothing, and rest and read. Yeah, their loss, but they don't understand that it is very much part of our culture."

He notices a definite feeling of separation when he's away overseas. New Zealanders, he feels, find it easy to get work, make friends and blend in wherever they go. "But on the down side we are still making it up as we go along, putting a bit of Kiwi DIY in to it. We have a different way of relating to each other that is peculiar to us, hard to define because we're in it, and I find that intriguing. I kind of like that naiveté. It is a natural state to be in if you're an artist who wants to come up with something brand new. I'm making no apologies for being a dumb fella from down under. I remember an Australian comedy skit I saw years ago where they were taking off Janet Frame, and they had these two girls with red fuzzy wigs sitting on overlarge chairs swinging their legs. That was such a New Zealand thing, swinging your legs and feeling a bit out of place and being oblivious to your naiveté. I think there is a humility about us that people don't understand. They know it's there but they don't know how to deal with it. Maybe it comes from being part of a close community."

Recently he was in London where he was involved with the opening of a New Zealand war memorial in Hyde Park. "It wasn't an ANZAC thing – it was purely for New Zealand. You know, I have difficulties believing that Australia is actually a Pacific nation, although it certainly has a Pacific influence. I tend to think it is less of a Pacific nation than New Zealand is, in terms of its generational culture. We're a lot friendlier … of course I'm biased.

"I've been lucky to spend a fair bit of time in England in the last couple

Dave Dobbyn

of years, and once I was visiting an art exhibition of new contemporary New Zealand artists at Cambridge University. A friend of mine had an installation there and she had a photo I had taken of my father's hands praying, a few days before he died. To go all that way and to find that photo staring back at me – suddenly the world shrank. It took the wind out of my Glenn Innes lungs."

While Dave suffers from homesickness when he is away he sees it as something to measure himself by. His somewhat unusual analogy goes deeper than most. "It's like being in the ocean and not knowing what monsters are lurking underneath. You're happily floating there and the weather is fine and you've got plenty of food, but who knows what's under there? If I'm working I'm fine, but I see homesickness as something you can get in touch with. I love discovering people doing their OE in London. People definitely discover their New Zealand-ness when they are away, what things are valuable and what aren't, and what the touchstones for your nationality are. It makes you ask all those questions such as who am I? As the Finns say, always take the weather with you, we're not here for long, so while carbon footprints aren't too much of an issue I'll get in while the going's good and as long as there's a gig I'll go. I'm dying to get to Antarctica at some point, going down there in the winter with just my guitar and Bible and see if I can come out with my marbles intact. I think there's something quite Catholic about that as an adventurous notion. I could come up with some really good songs. I don't look for oblivion any more. It's not worth chasing. In fact it's to be avoided at all costs!"

He remains disappointed about the levels of ignorance and racism in New Zealand, but is very excited about new models of living. "I have a feeling New Zealand will become in touch with itself again on a community level. We've woken up. I think we've learnt a lot in a short space of time and we're going to tell that story of what has happened in the last 20 years. I really feel that, as a songwriter, I need to describe Bastion Point, and describe the 1981 rugby tour – the things that have transformed us recently. It's going to take an awful lot to eradicate racism, but there are enough of us around to want to make that difference. It amazes me on one level how adaptable we are, and on the other how ignorant we can be when you see the divisions in race and religion. They're even talking about an underclass now, and the media take liberties and pigeonhole people.

"We seem to be in a continual state of realising how much we don't know. It's a healthy thing and it's exciting to see it in the arts and culture generally. People are telling their stories more now. If people are speaking from a non–violent level they can easily be heard."

He still wants to be an idealistic songwriter, and it helps him define himself and what songs can do to define an age. "Yeah, we have a dark side but we love that, I understand that there is that macabre attraction – I see it in the film-making. But I've also seen otherwise. I tend to lean towards the C.S. Lewis idea of perhaps we are pretty close to Narnia. It's a case of celebrating the light and that's what I'm in the business of celebrating. You can't shine the light unless you are immersed in the darkness – I discovered that while working on my last record. It's a personal choice to want to go there in the first place and want to write some songs out of it. You've got to become the warden and not the prisoner, as Bob Dylan says. As a song writer you can share an intimacy on a larger scale that also increases the boundaries of family and community. It's a blessing for me."

In 2000 Dave was invited to put music to one of James K. Baxter's poems for a compilation album, and admits at the time he felt out of his depth. "I thought, who am I dealing with? I once thought James K. Baxter was a loud-mouth drunk, but, you know, even at 15 I could see past that and know that he was a prophet. I was reading through all these poems of his, and this one poem leapt out at me. It was written in 1958 and called *Song of the Years*, and it hit me like a ton of bricks. This is part of the heritage we've got as true New Zealanders. It's my job to go into that history. I always love that about writing down place names.

"If you point to a place name you're pointing to its spirit. It's not just you naming a town. There are a whole lot of stories that go with it. That's the thing that I've woken up to in the last few years I've been travelling around New Zealand, it's an endless road. It's the joy of discovering it. I never get sick of it. And then I get on the stage in Eltham or some small town, and for a moment there I close my eyes and I think I just want this to last forever, I want to be doing this when I'm 95. Knowing all this is in my front yard – nothing can beat that. Sometimes I forget I'm a provincial person. Twenty years ago a lot of these towns were dead. Now there's a new life in them, and, you know, they all have good coffee now too! The cities are oblivious to what's going on, and unless you're out there I don't think you fully know what's going on in the country as a whole. So I feel hopeful. My heart is full of hope."